Starstruck

&

The No Boys Cricket Club

Starstruck

'A quirky comedy . . . soon darkens and mutates into a tragic vision of incestuous family life, soiled dreams and the rude wisdom of having to make a virtue of necessity.'
Evening Standard

The No Boys Cricket Club

'A fascinating psychological study of a woman coming face to face with her former self, gaining power from her cultural roots and eventually realising that the two distinct parts of her life make up a whole woman.' *What's On*

Roy Williams worked as an actor before turning to writing full-time in 1990. He graduated from Rose Bruford College in 1995 with a First Class BA Hons Degree in Writing. *The No Boys Cricket Club* won him a nomination for the TAPS Writer of the Year Award in 1996 and a nomination for New Writer of the Year by the Writers' Guild of Great Britain. He was the first recipient of the Alfred Fagon Award for *Starstruck* in 1997, which also won the John Whiting Award for the same year. His other plays include: *Josie's Boys* (Red Ladder Theatre Co.); *Night & Day* (Theatre Venture); *Homeboys*, which was broadcast as part of the Radio 4 First Bite Young Writers' Festival; and *Lift Off* (Royal Court Theatre Upstairs). Roy is currently writing *Portobello Road* for BBC TV, and is under commission to the Birmingham Rep and the Hampstead Theatre.

for a complete catalogue of Methuen Drama write to:

**Methuen Publishing Ltd
215 Vauxhall Bridge Road
London SW1V 1EJ**

STARSTRUCK

&

THE NO BOYS CRICKET CLUB

Roy Williams

Methuen

Published by Methuen 1999

1 3 5 7 9 10 8 6 4 2

First published in in the United Kingdom in 1999 by
Methuen Publishing Limited
215 Vauxhall Bridge Road, London, SW1V 2SA

Peribo Pty Ltd, 58 Beaumont Road, Mount Kuring-Gai
NSW 2080, Australia, ACN 002 273 761
(for Australia and New Zealand)

Random House South Africa (Pty) Limited
Endulini, 5a Jubilee Road, Parktown 2193, South Africa

Copyright © Roy Williams 1999

The right of Roy Williams to be identified as the author of this work has
been asserted by him in accordance with the Copyright, Designs and
Patents Act, 1988

Methuen Publishing Limited Reg. No. 3543167

A CIP catalogue record for this book is available from the British Library

ISBN 0 413 73810 8

Typeset by SX Composing DTP, Rayleigh, Essex
Printed and bound in Great Britain by
Cox & Wyman Ltd, Reading, Berkshire

Caution

Contents

Starstruck

Starstruck was first performed at the Tricycle Theatre, London, on 19 September 1998. The cast was as follows:

Hope	Adjoa Andoh
Wally	Nigel Clauzel
Dennis	Martin Cole
Young man/Lester	George Eggay
Pammy	Hannah Lawrence
Gravel	Eddie Nestor
Little Hope	Charis Thomas/Millicent Gezy

Directed by Indhu Rubasingham
Designed by Rosa Maggiora
Lighting by Jenny Kagan
Music by Fergus O'Hare

Characters

Hope, 38
Gravel, Hope's husband
Dennis, 19, Hope's son
Little Hope, 12, Hope's daughter
Young Man
Lester, a policeman
Pammy, Dennis's girlfriend
Wally, 22

The play is set in Kingston Town, Jamaica, in the 1970s.

Act One

Scene One

The Gilbey back yard. Morning. **Hope** *comes out from the house to take the washing off the line. She stops when she notices a battered old car that is in her yard.*

Hope (*furious*)   Oh Gravel! Is wat yu do now?

Kingston Bus Station. A young black man has just stepped off a bus, he enters carrying several large bags. He is struggling and looks around as if he is waiting for someone. **Dennis Gilbey** *is nearby. He watches the* **Young man** *carefully. He chooses the right time to approach him.*

Dennis   Yu awright young man?

Young man   Wat yu say?

Dennis   I ask if yu awright.

Young man   Me fine.

Dennis   Yu look like yu waitin' fer sumone.

Young man   Das my business.

Dennis   Awright man, easy nuh I juss bin friendly. Yu come down from country?

Young man   How yu know?

Dennis   Frankfield right? (**Young man** *nods.*) My mama come from Frankfield. Wat yer name? She might know yer family.

Young man   I am not givin' yu my name. My mama warned me about tief like yu . . .

Dennis   Is wat yu say man?

Young man   All yu town bwoys do is beg and tief fer money.

Dennis   Yu hear me beg yu? I don't wan' yer money. (*Takes out some notes from his pocket.*) See it deh. I juss waiting fer sumone like yu, he nuh here yet.

Young man   Yu don't wan' my money?

Dennis   No. Yu wan' cigarette?

Young man   Me mudda say I shouldn't smoke.

Dennis   I look like yer mudda man?

Young man *takes a cigarette,* **Dennis** *lights it for him, they enjoy their smoke.* **Young man** *coughs a bit.*

Dennis   Yu turnin' green man.

Young man (*panics*)   A lie yu tell.

Dennis   A joke me a mek. Wa' yer name?

Young man   Adrian.

Dennis   Pleased to meet yu Adrian. William. (*They shake hands.*) Deh yu see we not all tiefs, both our muddas come from country, an' dat mek me a country bwoy, yu tink I gonna tief from a country bwoy? No! So who yu waitin' fer?

Young man   My cousin Neil, im late.

Dennis   Neil?

Young man   Neil.

Dennis   Backside. So, it *yu* das Adrian!

Young man   Yes. Yu know me cousin?

Dennis   Yeah me know im. Tall right?

Young man   No man.

Dennis   Short?

Young man   No man.

Dennis   Medium height?

Young man   Yeah man.

Dennis   Yeah man me know im. Im work right?

Young man   Yeah I tink.

Dennis   Well he call me from work to say 'Dennis, go get me cousin fer me from de station ca' I have to work today'.

Young man   I tought yer name was William.

Dennis   And it is.

Young man   So why yu say yer name is Dennis?

Dennis   Dennis is my middle name, everyone call me Dennis.

Young man   So why yu tell me to call yu William?

Dennis   Adrian, calm yerself. All Neil asked me to do was put yu in a cab, mek sure yu don't get tief, ca' wat yer mudda says was right, plenty a thievin' wretches here. I not gonna tief yu. Awright, watch me now. (*Shouts.*) Cab! Over here man. See im comin', I go put in and mek sure im don't tief yu. Watch me now.

Cab driver, **Wally**, *enters.*

Wally   Who wan' de cab?

Dennis   My friend here.

Wally   Ware im goin'?

Young man   Taylor Street.

Wally   Me dunno ware dat is.

Dennis   Wat yu mean yu dunno?

Wally   Me dunno!

Dennis   Backside!

Wally   Yu wan' de cab or not?

Dennis   Come Adrian, show dis fool how to get deh.

Young man   My first time in Kingston.

Wally   Who wan' de cab?

Dennis   Hold on na Taylor Street, dat near Lambert's Field ain't it?

Wally   Me dunno.

Dennis   Well wat roads yu know?

Wally   Plenty!

Dennis   But not Taylor Street?

Wally   Cha me gone.

Dennis   Hold on. Wait. We're comin'. Come, Adrian, I help yu wid de bags.

Wally   Hold on a minute.

Dennis   Wat now?

Wally   Is wat yu mean 'we'?

Dennis   Two a we.

Wally   I can only tek one!

Dennis   I see yer car from here man, yu can tek two a we.

Wally   I got me tings in de back.

Dennis   Well fling yer tings out.

Wally   Look, last week my woman go throw me out.

Dennis   Come Adrian we go find another cab.

Wally   Hold on, I let yu pay half de fare. Half!

Dennis   Adrian? (**Adrian** *nods*.) Come!

Wally   Twenty dollar.

Young man   Here.

Dennis   Na man Adrian it awright. Neil give me money awready.

Dennis *gives* **Wally** *his money*.

Wally   Hey bwoy, bwoy? I say twenty dollar, not six.

Dennis   Is wat yu have in yer hand.

Wally   Six in me hand is wat me have.

Dennis   Yu can't count. (*Counts the notes.*)

Wally   Me wan' me money.

Dennis   Yer know wat happen, my gyal dis mornin' tell me she need money right, to buy food. I was in de toilet doin' my business so I juss say tek a lickle outta my wallet, de bitch mussa tek more dan half, I bet she come home wid a new dress.

Wally   Not my business if yer can't control your woman.

Dennis   At least I don't get fling out by she!

Wally   No money no cab!

Dennis   We go over to my friend Neil's. Im pay de rest.

Wally   Look bwoy, me I bin living on dis Island fer too long. I wan' twenty dollar. Read my lips, hear it come out, twenty dollar, twenty dollar, twenty dollar . . .

Dennis   Give de blasted man im money Adrian. Don't worry I tell Neil, we'll get de money back.

Wally   Right, mek up your mind who comin'.

Dennis   Adrian yu go.

Wally   Yu nuh hear de boy say im don't know ware de place is?

Dennis   I come wid yu first den, show you de way.

Wally   Hold on a minute.

Dennis   Wat now?

Wally   Yer gonna leave im here alone? What if someone come and try and tief im tings?

Dennis   It not far.

Young man   Maybe I can walk den.

Dennis/Wally   No!

Young man   Wat?

Dennis   Wat I mean is, it not far by car. But walking wid dem bags? No. Yu get sum good fer nuttin bwoy trying to tief it off yu, and I promise Neil I won't let nuttin 'appen to yu. Yu got room fer de bags here.

Wally   Come! (*Takes the bags and exits.*)

Young man   Hey!

Dennis   Adrian, rest yerself. (*Examines him.*) Tek your jacket off, off man! (**Adrian** *obeys, he hands it over.*) And yer tie. Now roll up yer sleeves. Unbutton de top a your shirt, show a bit a chest. Deh. Yu look like a Kingston bwoy now. Keep yer hands in yer pockets and walk around like so.

Dennis *struts around to show him.*

Dennis   Try it.

Adrian *copies* **Dennis**. *He is not as good as* **Dennis**, *who is trying very hard not to laugh.*

Dennis   Bit more strut Adrian. Swing yer hip.

Young man   Like dis.

Dennis   Yeah man.

Young man   Yu sure Kingston bwoys walk like dis?

Dennis   Alla dem. (*Car horn beeps.*) Back soon yeah. Strut Adrian strut!

Dennis *dashes off.* **Young man** *looks very confused. He is unsure what to do. He remembers the steps to strut. He begins to enjoy himself as he slowly gets the hang of it. Suddenly the penny drops.*

Young man   Police!

An alley. **Dennis** *and* **Wally** *are laughing their heads off. The* **Young man**'s *bags are emptied and contents scattered all over the* *floor.* **Dennis** *mimics the* **Young man***'s attempts to strut; the boys laugh even more.*

Dennis   So he goes, 'yu mean like dis?'

Wally   Bwoy stupid, more stupid than dat fool fool gyal last week, remember?

Dennis *(going through the bags)*   Yu wan' mango?

Wally   Throw it here. So, how much we tek?

Dennis   Sixty dollar.

Wally   Joey's bar?

Dennis   Yeah man.

Pammy *(offstage)*   Dennis!

Wally   Jesus!

Dennis   Pammy.

Wally   Tell her to go man.

Dennis   Awright.

Pammy *enters.*

Dennis   Wa' 'appening Princess, yer awright?

Pammy   No bodder princess me right, juss no bodder.

Dennis   Rahtid, is wat me do now?

Pammy   Wat yu do? Tink Dennis, tink.

Dennis   Oh lord.

Pammy   Yes!

Dennis   I was supposed to meet yu at work right . . .

Pammy   I is not a dog Dennis.

Dennis   Pammy! Is when yu ever hear me call yu a dog?

Pammy   Don't keep me waitin' den.

Dennis   Yu my princess.

Pammy   And don't even bodder wid dat. Move.

Dennis   Smile gyal. Look, I mek money today.

Pammy   Who yu steal from now?

Dennis   Look nuh, thirty dollar!

Pammy (*snatches it*)   Dat can go to de fifty yu owe me awready.

Dennis   Hey! We wan' go Joey's bar.

Pammy   Too bad.

Wally   Give de man back im money gyal.

Pammy   Who ask yu?

Dennis   Sweetiepie?

Pammy   No.

Dennis   Honeybuns?

Pammy   No.

Dennis   Yu really tink dis gonna stop me going out wid Wally?

Pammy   Yes. Later.

Wally   Bwoy yu juss gonna stand deh and let . . .

Dennis   Hold on. (*Quotes.*) 'Oh, she doth teach the torches to burn bright! It seems she hangs upon the cheek of night.'

Wally   Wat!

Pammy   Stop it Dennis.

Dennis   'As a rich jewel in Ethiop's ear, beauty too rich for use for earth too dear! Did my heart love till now? Forswear it sight! For I never saw true beauty till this night.'

Pammy (*seriously aroused*)   Move.

Dennis *holds her in his arms and kisses her.* **Wally** *laughs to himself, then out loud when he sees* **Dennis** *take the money out of* **Pammy**'s *hand with great ease.*

Wally   Gw'n Dennis!

Dennis   Come!

Pammy   Yer wort'less wretch!

Dennis   I call yu later Pammy.

Pammy   'Bout yer tink yu can sweet talk me. Deh's plenty oder bwoys who wan' sweet talk me.

Wally   We know all about yu and dem oder bwoys Pammy.

Dennis   Wat oder bwoys?

Pammy   Tommy Riley fer one.

Dennis   Dat frog-eyed fool!

Pammy   Dat frog-eyed fool have a job, im have a car. He even offer to tek me to a dance on Saturday. I can call im any time I like.

Dennis   Well I don't like. Yu my woman Pammy Simpson.

Pammy   Yu never tek me out.

Dennis   Yu wan' go dance, I tek yu.

Pammy   Come Saturday you lose all yer money. Yu and dis fool.

Wally   Hey!

Pammy   Hey wat!

Dennis   Yu really tink I enjoy sitting down doing nuttin?

Pammy   Cha Dennis juss ferget 'bout it right. All yu do is act up and play de fool. If yu love it so much go show it to dem flim people, ca' me tired a it. Me sick an' tired a it.

Dennis   Wat flim people?

Pammy   Yu know man.

Dennis   No.

Wally   Come on Dennis, leave de gyal.

Dennis   Wait nuh.

Pammy   Yu really mean yu don't know?

Dennis   Wat flim people Pammy?

Pammy (*acting all coy*)   Nuttin.

Dennis   Pammy?

Pammy   It nuttin.

Dennis   Pamela?

Pammy   Forget it.

Dennis   Wat flim? Hollywood flim?

Wally   Shut up man.

Dennis   It is right?

Pammy   Maybe. Maybe not.

Dennis   Tell me.

Pammy   I tink about it.

Dennis   Tell me now!

Pammy   Walk wid me on de beach an' I consider it.

Dennis   It have stars right?

Wally   Bwoy don't beg, can't yu see dat she . . .

Dennis   Pammy!

Pammy   Yu go walk me to de beach? See yu later den.

Dennis (*tickles her*)   Wat flim people Pamela?

Pammy   A whole heap a white people arrive in de hotel de oder day to mek sum flim.

Dennis   Ware?

Pammy   All over town. But I see sum a dem down by Lambert Street today, outside Miss Stuart's shop.

Dennis   Who star in it, yu find out? (*Goes to tickle her again.*)

Pammy   Granger!

Dennis   Granger? Stewart Granger?

Pammy   Yes!

Dennis   Jesus Christ man! Stewart Granger!

Wally   Im an actor right?

Dennis   Movie star! 'Bout actor? Dis mus' be sum big flim de mekin' if deh have im. Oh Pammy, it come – dis is my chance!

Wally   Wat im say now?

Pammy   Yu mean he nuh tell yu? Fool wan' be an actor.

Dennis   Movie star! Wait till I tell Mama.

Pammy   Deh not lookin' fer any actors man, deh got de own.

Dennis   Shut up man, deh mus wan' people to stand in de background, create the right kind a atmosphere, mek people believe deh really in Jamaica. Well, that is me, is it not?

Pammy   I tought yu knew.

Dennis   I bin busy.

Pammy   Busy tiefin'. I should kep' my mout shut.

Dennis   But such a lovely mout. Yu wan' me to get a job, I goin' get a job. I gonna be famous gyal.

Pammy   Save it fer de police.

Dennis Why?

Pammy   Oh didn't I mention? Lester lookin' fer de two a yu.

Wally   Rass! Come on Dennis. Leave de case man.

Dennis   It made a leader! Hold it fer me Pammy.

Pammy   Oh no.

Dennis   Come on.

Pammy   I hate yu Dennis Gilbey!

They run.

The yard. **Hope** *peeling potatoes.* **Little Hope** *climbs over the fence and jumps into the yard. Her dress is torn and her face is bleeding. She tries to sneak into the house without being seen.*

Hope   Lickle Hope Gilbey!

Little Hope *freezes.*

Hope   I hope dat not yu tryin' to sneak into de house.

Little Hope   No Mama. How yu know it was me?

Hope   I got eyes in de back a my head. (*Turns round.*) Look at de state a yer dress chile. Is wat yu bin doing?

Little Hope   Nuttin.

Hope   Yu wan' fer me to get de belt?

Little Hope   No Mama.

Hope   So yu gonna tell me wat 'appen?

Little Hope   Yes Mama.

Hope   Gw'n den.

Little Hope   It was Billy Walker.

Hope   Billy Walker? Im a big bwoy, Lickle Hope. Wat yu doin' fighting im?

Little Hope   I kick im in de face im have blood all over im shirt.

Hope   Stop dat talk.

Little Hope   Im call Daddy a retard.

Hope   Don't say dat word.

Little Hope   I didn't, Billy Walker say it.

Hope   Yu don't have to repeat it.

Little Hope   I tell im to tek it back but im say no.

Hope   So yu kick im in de face?

Little Hope   Yes. I don' wan' no one mekin' fun a Daddy.

Hope   Sure yu weren't rolling around in de dirt again?

Little Hope   It de trut Mama.

Hope   I hope so. Ca' yu an' me are gonna pay Billy's mudda a visit. And yu go say sorry, right?

Little Hope   Yes Mama.

Hope   Fighting like sum dog, yu don't feel shame? Look at yer dress.

Little Hope   Yu have to throw it away now.

Hope   Oh no. Yu gonna be wearing dis dress again , I promise yu dat. Yu pikne love to tink we got money to burn. I don't wan' to hear any more stories about yu fightin' yer hearin' me? Yu is a young lady Lickle Hope. Time fer yu to start acting like one.

Little Hope   But wat if deh start mekin' fun a Daddy . . .

Hope   It not yer concern.

Little Hope   We got a new car Mama?

Hope   No.

Little Hope   So wat it doing here?

Hope   It going right back ware it come from.

Little Hope   Has Daddy done a stupid ting again Mama?

Hope   I told yu it not yer concern.

Gravel *whistles a tune offstage.*

Little Hope (*beaming*)   It Daddy!

Hope   Gw'n inside and clean up.

Little Hope *does as she is told.* **Gravel** *enters the yard. He looks very pleased when he sees the car.*

Hope   Yu late.

Gravel   Bunch a fools carry on like dog, following de white man.

Hope   Wat yu chat 'bout now?

Gravel   Nuttin. Dinner ready?

Hope   It soon come.

Gravel   It here! It here at last Hope.

Hope   I got eyes yu nuh Gravel.

Gravel   I know wat yu gonna say.

Hope   Do yu now?

Gravel   And yu right. No way is dis ole piece a junk worth wat Ned Williams was offering. But im knock off half de price Hope. Half price!

Hope   Oh Gravel man!

Gravel   Gravel couldn't turn it away.

Hope   Yes im could.

Gravel   Our own car.

Hope   Look at de state a it.

Gravel   Yu tink he con Gravel?

Hope   Hasn't he?

Gravel   Dis my dream.

Hope   It goin' back ware it came from, and yu goin' get yer money back off Ned Williams yer hearing me?

Gravel   The car is staying right ware it is Hope, de money is staying ware it is, in Ned Williams back pocket, yu hearing me?

Hope   Yu wan' fer dem to laugh?

Gravel   No one laughin' at Gravel.

Hope   So how come yer own daughter come home with blood all over her face ca' she fighting sum bwoy who calling yu names?

Gravel   Yu tink Gravel boddered by wat a child have to say? Listen to me. (*Pitches it.*) Gravel & Son! The business. Cab business. See how full de bus get lately?

Hope   Brewster got im cab company down de road man.

Gravel   Brewster tell me de oder day he gettin' out. Im hire six drivers last month an' every one a dem run off wid im money.

Hope   Man love to moan, don't mean im ready to sell up.

Gravel   Gravel fix up de car, tek it out on de road, mek sum money, den we go out buy anudda one, do de same ting. We'll be rich!

Hope   Like we be rich having our own boat, like we be rich running our own shop . . .

Gravel   Oh shush.

Hope   Yu have a job.

Gravel   Gravel too good to be packin' bananas all im life.

Hope   Now yu sound like yer own son, ambition fer de young Gravel. How yu know yer can fix de damn ting.

Gravel   Dis is wat Gravel meant to do.

Hope   Twenty dollar say Dennis won't drive cab fer yu.

Gravel   Wat dis have to do wid Dennis please?

Hope   Gravel & Son?

Gravel   Gravel Senior, me daddy. Dennis can find im own job.

Little Hope, *now dressed in t-shirt and pants, comes running out of the house.*

Little Hope   Daddy!

Gravel   Hey!

Hope   Wat yer running fer chile?

Gravel   Gravel miss dis face yu see!

Little Hope   Can I play in de car Daddy?

Hope   It look like toy to yu?

Gravel   Gw'n.

Hope   Den yu can set de table.

Little Hope *jumps in, gets behind the steering wheel and pretends to drive.*

Hope   De bwoy a lot like yu nuh.

Gravel   Gravel no tief.

Hope   Yeah, see de worse in im again.

At this point, **Dennis** *climbs over the yard fence and falls over.*

Hope   But Jesus Christ.

Gravel   Yu were saying?

Hope   Wa wrong wid yu children? Use de door!

Dennis   Mama yer nuh see me right.

Hope   Dennis?

Lester (*offstage*)   Gilbey!

Dennis *tries to hide in the car.*

Gravel   Oh no.

Dennis   Come on Pops.

Gravel   Out!

Dennis *dives into the chicken shed and hides.*

Little Hope (*laughing, chanting*)   Dennis in de chicken shed, Dennis in de chicken shed . . .

Hope   Quiet gyal!

Hope *shields* **Dennis** *as* **Lester** *enters.*

Lester (*out of breath*)   Yu wan' tell me ware he is?

Hope   Where's who?

Lester   Gil . . . Gilbey!

Hope   Im not here. (**Lester** *looks around.*) Why yer can' leave im alone Lester?

Lester   I was chasin' im . . . (*Unable to say any more.*)

Hope   Oh sit down man!

Gravel (*gets a stool for* **Lester**)   Here Lester.

Hope   Yu fat . . .

Gravel   Hope!

Lester   Wat yu standin' deh fer? (*Stands up.*) Stand aside please.

Hope   Yu think I stupid enough to hide my own son in a chicken shed?

Lester   Come outta deh Gilbey.

Hope   Yu deaf?

Gravel   Awright, everyone juss calm down awright. Come Lester yu wan' to tell me wat dis is all about.

Lester   Im and dat nephew a yours, and sum gyal. Deh got dis poor bwoy from de country, dem tek all im tings.

Hope   Straight away yu know it Dennis.

Lester   Im done it before. (*Shouts at the shed.*) Yu got five seconds!

Gravel   Come Lester, we work summin out.

Lester   Wat we have to work out?

Gravel   Come see wat Gravel got, come. Come out a deh Little Hope. Wat yu tink? Lickle bit a paint,

Little Hope   I wanna paint it!

Gravel   . . . work on de engine, cab business!

Lester   Wat about Brewster?

Gravel   Brewster gone man. Look inside nuh man. Gravel gonna put nice velvet seats. Mek it look comfortable.

Lester   It gonna look good.

Gravel *takes out a bottle of rum from his tool box.*

Gravel   So anyway, how's yer daddy Lester, im awright?

Lester (*tempted*)   Im fine.

Gravel   Tell im Gravel say how'd yu do.

Lester (*takes the bottle*)   Last time Gravel, it has to be. (*To the chicken shed.*) Yu is a lucky fool Dennis. (*Exit.*)

Gravel   Take care Lester. Yu plannin' on staying in dat shed all day?

Dennis *comes out covered in straw.*

Gravel   In all our born days, we have never had a tief in de family till yu come outta yer mudda.

Dennis   We never had anyting in all our born days!

Gravel   Not even man enough to say sorry.

Dennis (*insincere*)   Sorry.

Gravel   Lie!

Dennis   Awright me not sorry.

Gravel   See how selfish he is.

Dennis   Mek up yer mind man, wat yu wan' me to say?

Gravel   I mek up my mind an' fling yer arse out.

Hope   Gravel calm yerself.

Gravel   Yu aways defending im.

Hope   I'm not, I wan' yu to stay calm. (*She slaps* **Dennis** *across the head.*)

Dennis   Mama? See how deh treat me Little Hope?

Hope   No jokes.

Little Hope (*enjoying this*)   Dennis get licks!

Hope   Go inside and set de table.

Little Hope *goes inside.* **Dennis** *follows her.*

Gravel   Gravel not finish wid yu yet. Yu don't tink it time yu stop farmin' de arse wid yerself?

Dennis   Yu mean like yu? A cab business?

Gravel   Wat wrong wid dat?

Dennis (*to* **Hope**)   Im not go learn, I tell yu awready . . .

Gravel   I ask yu a question, wat wrong wid dat? My fudda were a cab driver, my broder was a cab driver.

Dennis   Yeah, Grandaddy die old an' broke, Uncle Neville run off to Englan'.

Gravel Maybe yu would like to fly away to Englan' den, that suit yu?

Dennis Suited yu.

Gravel Come juss like Neville.

Hope Don't.

Gravel Tief off yer own juss like de white man.

Dennis Dem country fools not my own right, I'm my own!

Hope I go bus' two heads in a minute.

Dennis Yeah but . . .

Gravel . . . An' he aways . . .

Hope Stop.

Gravel *goes to his car.* **Hope** *walks over to him.*

Gravel Wat yu wan'?

Hope Ware dat bokkle a rum come from?

Gravel It was juss a bottle, bin lyin' round.

Hope It look like a new bottle to me. Gravel?

Gravel Wat yu wan'?

Hope Yu come like a blasted child. Yu know wat de doctor say . . .

Gravel Wat de hell im know?

Hope More than yu.

Gravel Gravel go fer im dinner. (*Goes in.*)

Dennis (*mimics his father*) 'Wat de hell im know?'

Hope Dennis?

Dennis 'Gravel go fer im dinner.'

Hope *clouts him around the head again.*

Dennis   Mama!

Hope   Enough.

Dennis   Midas.

Hope (*raises her hand*)   Yer wan' anudda one? Stop calling im dat.

Dennis   It 'appening all over again Mama.

Hope   I know.

Dennis   An' we're de ones dat have to sort it out.

Hope   No Dennis, I'm de one dat have to sort it out.

Dennis   Hey, Mama? Who win de Best Actor Oscar in 1954?

Hope   I'm not in de mood.

Dennis   Yu angry wid me?

Hope   Yu promised me yu stop tiefing.

Dennis   Wally hard up man, he need money.

Hope   Is Wally go help yu when yer arse thrown in jail?

Dennis   But dem country fools mek it so easy fer us, deh so stupid man. Yu shoulda seen me Mama, I was so good . . .

Hope   Yu fudda come from country.

Dennis   Exactly.

Hope   Tek that smile right off yer face young man. I mean it. Who was de gyal?

Dennis   Pammy.

Hope   Is she who rope yu into dis.

Dennis   Mama don't talk to me like I'm Pops, right?

Hope   Yer not mekin' tings easy Dennis. I gotta deal wid yer fudda, I can't deal wid yu at de same time.

Dennis　Awright!

Hope　Bwoy yu is too good fer tiefing.

Dennis　I'm special.

Hope　Right.

Dennis　I bet I know wat can mek yu smile.

Hope　I'm not one a yer gyals yu know bwoy.

Dennis　Yu don't know.

Hope　Know wat?

Dennis　Who star in *Waterloo Road*?

Hope　Dennis!

Dennis　Who!

Hope　Stewart Granger a course. Why yu ask?

Dennis　Juss wondered.

Hope　Yu said it mek me smile. Wa' goin' on?

Dennis　Yu really wan' to know?

Hope　Yes.

Dennis　Yu sure 'bout dis?

Hope　Dennis!

Dennis　Yu best sit down den.

Hope　Yer mudda fine ware she is.

Dennis　Awright. Dinner smell good, maybe I should eat summin before . . .

Hope　So yu wan' me to beat yu?

Dennis　Awright, guess who starring in sum flim dem Hollywood people mekin' right here?

Hope　Wat?

Dennis   Come on, guess.

Hope   How de hell should I know, I didn't even know deh mekin' sum flim . . .

Dennis   Mama, yu juss said im name.

Hope (*not wanting to believe it*)   Shut up.

Dennis   No joke.

Hope   Yu tink me fool?

Dennis   It Pammy who tell me Mama. Im stayin' at de hotel ware she work. He's here.

Hope   Stewart Granger?

Dennis   Yep.

Hope   On dis island?

Dennis   Yep!

Hope (*ecstatic*)   Jesus Christ. Jesus Christ! Oh Lord, oh God . . .

Dennis   Yu wan' sit down?

Hope   Ware?

Dennis   Juss on de steps.

Hope   No yu fool, ware?

Dennis (*teasing*)   Nearby.

Hope (*like a little girl*)   Don't tease me right!

Dennis   Outside Miss Stuart's shop.

Hope   Backside! (*Runs out of the yard.*) Dennis I can't see nuttin man.

Dennis   So let's go deh.

Hope   Yes, no. Dennis go in yer fudda's shed, get me im binocular.

Dennis *goes.* **Hope** *climbs on the hood of the car.*

Hope (*impatient*)   Wat yu waitin' fer, rain?

Dennis (*coming out with the binoculars*)   Yu nuh answer my question yet?

Hope   Wat yu chat 'bout?

Dennis   Who win de Best Actor Oscar in 1954 . . .

Hope   Marlon Brando!

Dennis   For?

Hope   *On the Waterfront!* (*Holds out her hand for the binoculars.*)

Dennis   And who win it in 1955 . . .

Hope   Yu wan' eat in dis house?

Dennis *laughs as he throws her the binoculars. He joins her on top of the car.*

Hope   I aways knew he'd come here. Man bin all over de world mekin' flims, why shouldn't he come here?

Dennis   Well im here now.

Hope   Deh he is, oh my God, Stewart Granger!

Dennis (*looks through binoculars*)   Ware?

Hope (*pointing*)   Deh. Look, im sittin' down in im chair right, wid im sunglasses.

Dennis   Ware?

Hope   Deh bwoy, yu blind?

Dennis   No, but me can't see im.

Hope   Im de only one sittin' down. Dennis, look, see how everyone else runnin' round, wid all dem lights and camera and ting?

Dennis   Yeah. Das not im Mama.

Hope   Yu mus' be blind. It im Dennis, he look de same as he did in *Beau Brummel*, tall, jet black hair . . .

Dennis   Mama, it not im.

Hope   Oh quiet, who ask yu anyhow?

Dennis   Awright.

Hope (*looks again*)   Yer right. It not Stewart Granger, so who it den?

Dennis   Me dunno. (*Takes the binoculars.*) Hey, who dat comin' outta de car? Raquel Welch!

Hope   Das not her Dennis.

Dennis   It look like her. She got same hair, same legs, every ting!

Hope   Close yer mout son.

Dennis   She look nice.

Hope   So ware her tits?

Dennis   Mama!

Hope   Gal ain't got no tits. Yu see dem? I see more tit on a dog. (**Dennis** *wants the binoculars.*) Move yerself.

Wally *enters the yard.*

Wally   Gilbey bwoy!

Dennis   Wa gw'n!

Wally   Hello Auntie.

Hope   Walford.

Dennis   Wally, tell Mama who dat woman is fer me please.

Wally   I dunno, but she look like Raquel Welch.

Dennis   It is Raquel Welch.

Wally   Na man.

Hope   Tank you!

Wally   Too short. All de same I wouldn't mind grind dat.

Hope   Excuse me?

Wally   I wouldn't mind actin' wid her dass wat I mean.

Hope   I know wat yu mean.

Wally   Sorry Auntie.

Dennis   Since when yu wan' act?

Wally   Well if yu wan' to do it . . .

Dennis   If deh's any part, it mine.

Wally   Deh's room fer more dan juss yu yer nuh Dennis. Or yu tink I is better dan yu?

Dennis   Yu stay which part yu deh. I go get closer, show dem wat I can do, right?

Hope   Hold on a minute. (*Brushes* **Dennis**'s *hair with her hands, and his shirt.*)

Dennis   Mama?

Hope   I don't wan yu goin' down deh, lookin' all rough.

Dennis   I go miss out.

Hope   Good luck. And hey, yu behave yerself.

Dennis   I go come back a star Mama. Hey 1962, who win Best Actor?

Hope   Gregory Peck.

Dennis (*leaving*)   Wat flim?

Hope (*calls*)   *To Kill a Mockingbird*!

Wally   So how's tings Auntie?

Hope   Fine, Walford.

Wally   Uncle Gravel angry wid me?

Hope   I wouldn't stay too long if I were yu. If Dennis see Stewart Granger he better get me im autograph.

Wally   Dat old man.

Hope   Dat old man can teach yu a lot.

Wally   Like wat?

Hope   How to treat a woman good, mek her feel like a lady. How to talk right, stand up straight. Every ting im wan', im get.

Wally   Nuttin wrong wid de way me talk.

Hope   Yu island men all de same, can't see furder than yer own nosehole.

Wally   Im juss a man like me yu know Auntie.

Hope   He is a gentleman. Believe me, dis island could do wid more gentlemen.

Wally   Im not yer type.

Hope   So wat is my type den Walford?

Wally *rubs his hands up and down her thigh.* **Hope** *looks like she is enjoying it.* **Wally** *then thrusts his hand up her skirt.*

Hope   Ease up nuh. Stop it! Yu wan' do it out here?

Wally   Why not?

Hope   Yer Uncle Gravel come out any minute, yu mad?

Wally   Yu like living dangerously.

Hope   No!

Wally   I nuh see yu fer weeks.

Hope   Yu get too crazy Walford.

Wally   Auntie, yu mek me crazy.

Hope   Stop! (*Climbs down.*)

Wally   Come round de corner.

Hope   I look like whore to yu?

Wally   One minute.

Hope   I haven't got a minute. Gravel only inside man.

Wally   Leave im, leave wid im toy.

Hope   Wat yu mean by dat? Walford?

Wally   I bump into Ned, he tell how much Gravel pay fer dis. (*Laughs.*)

Hope   It not funny.

Wally   Everyting dat fool do is funny. Ned bin trying to get rid a dis fer months. No one would touch it, 'cept Gravel. Hey come on.

Hope   I don't wan' yu.

Wally   Oh man, don't play dis game again.

Hope   I'm not playing. Yu not gettin' nuttin outta me Walford till yu tell yer friend Ned I go be callin' on im.

Wally   Not even a feel?

Hope   No.

Wally   Suck on yer tittie?

Hope   Juss tell im I wan' im to buy de car back.

Wally   Yu mus be jokin'!

Hope   My face tell yu I jokin'? I wan' im to pay double wat Gravel give im. (**Wally** *laughs.*) So he can mek up any story he like, so long as he mek it good.

Wally   Ned won't go fer dat.

Hope   Ned have no choice.

Wally   Wat yu mean?

Hope   Let's juss say im wife wouldn't like it.

Wally   Yu sleeping wid im?

Hope   And wat if I were?

Wally   I wouldn't like it.

Hope   Yu don't own me Wally. No one own me. I'm not sleeping wid im. But me know who is.

Wally   Who?

Hope   Dat fer me to know, and im wife to find out if he don't play ball.

Wally   All dis fer Gravel Gilbey.

Hope   No one cons my husband and gets away wid it right? I'm sick a everyone laughin' at im.

Wally   Awright. But wat in it fer me?

Hope   Soon Walford.

Wally   Yu wan' drive me mad?

Hope   Calm yerself. Jesus! Lickle bit a fun an' yu get all excited.

Wally   Come away wid me.

Hope   Yu don't listen.

Wally   We go live in Spanish Town yeah?

Hope   Yu really do that?

Wally   I'd do any ting fer yu.

Hope   Stop talkin' like a fool Wally.

Wally   My fault me love yu?

Hope   Yu love me? Bwoy yu nuh tink I never hear dat before?

Wally   I mean it.

Hope   Say it again den.

Wally   I love yu Hope.

Hope   Say 'yer the only ting worth stayin' fer on dis island, Hope Kiffin'.

Wally   Yer the only ting worth stayin' fer on dis island, Hope Kiffin.

Hope *shakes her head.*

Wally   Who was I supposed to be?

Hope   No mind.

Wally   Who?

Hope   Juss tell everyone to leave my husban' alone right? Im not lazy like yu, im have a job.

Wally   Had a job, im a leave.

Hope   No, im only say he going to leave.

Wally   Im a leave. Yu know Thurston who work wid im right? I hear im say Uncle and de boss a dat factory have a big argument. Boss say im pack box wrong, Gravel call im an ejut – right in front a everybody.

Hope (*angry*)   Gravel!

Wally   He nuh even tell im own wife de trut.

Hope (*snaps*)   Every day it summin, every blasted day it aways summin!

Wally   Ease up.

Hope   I don't wan' to ease up. I juss wan' . . .

Wally   Wat?

Hope   Never mind.

Wally   Tek yer mind off tings fer a minute. Relax, have sum fun. Den I tell Ned, I promise yu. Feel my ting. Feel it.

Gravel *comes out of the house. He sees them.*

Hope   It gettin' big. No Wally wait, wait! Come round corner.

Hope *and* **Wally** *disappear behind the yard fence.* **Gravel** *watches them leave. He goes over to his car and lifts up the bonnet.*

Gravel   Watch me now, Pops.

Scene Two

The next day. **Dennis** *and* **Pammy** *are in the yard.*

Dennis   '. . . She speaks. Yet she says nothing. What of that? Her eye discourses. I will answer it. I am too bold, 'tis not to me she speaks. Two of the fairest stars in all the heaven, having some business, do entreat her eyes to twinkle in their spheres till thcy return. What if her eyes were there, they in her head? The brightness of her cheek would shame those stars as daylight doth a lamp.' (*To* **Pammy**.) Excited?

Pammy   Maybe.

Dennis   Yu wan' come inside?

Pammy   No.

Dennis   All me ever hear from yu is no.

Pammy   An' yu go go on hearing it.

Dennis   We go marry anyway.

Pammy   I nuh see no ring on my finger.

Dennis   Yu know we go do it?

Pammy   When?

Dennis   Soon. So we might as well, yu know.

Pammy   No.

Dennis   I can't remember de las time I have de house to myself. I know yu wan' to. I can tell.

Pammy   Oh yes?

Dennis   'Her eyes in heaven would through the airy region stream so bright that birds would sing and think it were not right. See how she leans her cheek upon her hand! Oh that I were a glove upon her hand! That I might touch that cheek!'

Pammy   Nuttin but rubbish!

Dennis   Rubbish? Dis is Shakespeare gyal. Romeo pouring out im heart to Juliet, only gyal im love in de whole world, fool dead fer her. It romance. Yu don't wan' romance Pammy?

Pammy   Oh I wan' it.

Dennis (*glad*)   Good.

Pammy   Togeder with marriage, house, and pikne.

Dennis   Maybe I should go check yer mudda. I bet she coulda mek me happy.

Pammy *kicks him hard*.

Dennis   Ow! Easy nuh Pammy.

Pammy   Don't tell me 'bout easy.

Dennis   Will yu stop kicking me, please?

Pammy   Yu wan' my mama so bad? Go den. She at home waitin' fer yu, and de rest of a whole line a men wid thirty dollar in deh pocket . . . Go if das wat yer . . . (**Dennis** *grabs her foot just as she tries to kick him again*.) Let go a my foot.

Dennis   Yer mean dis foot?

Pammy   Let go.

Dennis (*strokes her foot*)   Skin smooth. (*Sniffs*.) Feet stink!

Pammy   I hate yu!

Dennis   No yu don'.

Pammy   Yu mek me sick.

Dennis   Yu love me, yu can't stop dreamin' about me.

Pammy   Let me go now!

Dennis   Calm down. I was juss tryin' to mek yu jealous like yu did wid me when yu say Tommy Riley wan'ed to . . .

Pammy   Forget Tommy Riley. Yu really tink I coulda interest in dat frog-eyed fool? Nuh smile at me.

Dennis   I love yu Pammy.

Pammy   Yeah, when yer wan' summin. Yu don't wan fer marry me.

Dennis   Who say I don't?

Pammy   Yu nuh even find job yet.

Dennis   I'm workin' on it. It my fault dem flim people tell me de don' wan' me?

Pammy   Shut up about de flim man.

Dennis   I can act, Pammy.

Pammy   Dem never tink so.

Dennis   Dem never give a chance, all dem say is 'move'.

Pammy   I don't wan' to be married to an actor, hear me now, I wan' be married to a man dat go look after me.

Dennis   I can do both. Yu an' me are go live in a big house, Pammy Simpson. I tellin' yu.

Pammy   And in de mean time?

Dennis   I dunno Pammy.

Pammy (*mimics*)   I dunno Pammy!

Dennis   Wat yer have to ruin de dream fer?

Pammy   Ca' yu can't live on dreams.

Dennis   But wat if yu could? Wat if all yu had to do snap yer fingers, and watever yu wan', yu get. Yu tellin' me de world wouldn't be a better place if dat were so?

Pammy   I dunno Dennis.

Dennis (*mimics*)   I dunno Dennis.

Pammy   Dreams are in yer head fool, ware deh supposed to be. Stop playin' de arse and go back to work.

Dennis   Too late. Factory job gone.

Pammy   Work fer yer pops den.

Dennis   Work fer Midas? Everything im touch turn to shit.

Pammy   I tink it a good idea. Yu see how full de bus get lately?

Dennis   Two months me give im.

Pammy   Don't mek fun a im.

Dennis   It all I can do. I can't yell at de man in case im get all work up and have anudda heart attack. It my fault im sick, im aways sick.

Pammy   Yu don't know how lucky yu are, havin' a fudda.

Dennis   Sorry Mama.

Pammy   I wish I was yu nuh, give yu two licks in yer head.

Dennis   I not askin' Midas fer nuttin Pammy.

Pammy   It go kill yu?

Dennis   Yu are so good ain't it, wan' to look after everybody, Pammy Simpson.

Pammy   Yu wait till we marry. Gonna put yu under serious manners. Dennis Gilbey.

Dennis (*aroused*)   Can' wait.

Pammy   Best speak to yer fudda den.

Dennis   Awright. But yu can't do a lickle summin fer me now?

Pammy *undoes the top buttons on her blouse.*

Pammy   Juss a feel.

Dennis *puts his hands down* **Pammy**'s *blouse.* **Pammy** *moves her head as* **Dennis** *tries to kiss her.*

Dennis   Tiny lickle kiss?

Pammy *lets him kiss her.* **Little Hope** *enters, carrying bags of shopping. She giggles to herself as she watches* **Dennis** *and* **Pammy**.

Little Hope   Gw'n Dennis!

Dennis *and* **Pammy** *look up.*

Dennis   Little Hope!

Little Hope   I know wat yu bin doin'.

Dennis   No yu don't.

Little Hope   Grindin'! (*Thrusts her pelvis back and forth.*)

Dennis   Lickle scamp, come here!

Little Hope (*chanting*)   No! Dennis grindin' Pammy, Dennis grindin' Pammy . . .

Dennis   Come here before, I go gobble yu all up!

Little Hope (*still laughing*)   No!

Dennis *chases his sister into the house.* **Hope** *enters the yard carrying bags of shopping.*

Hope   Wass all de blasted noise in here? (*Clocks* **Pammy**.)

Pammy (*cold*)   Mrs Gilbey.

Hope (*even colder*)   Pamela.

Pammy   Yu wan' help wid those?

Hope   I can manage. (*Sees the shopping* **Little Hope** *has put on the ground.*) Lickle Hope? Why yu nuh put de shopping away like I tell yu to? (*Shouts.*) Lickle Hope?

Pammy   She not across de street yu nuh.

Hope (*shouting again*)   Little Hope!

Little Hope *runs out chased by* **Dennis**.

Hope   Little Hope, don't mek me chase yu. Tek de shopping inside like me tell yu to. Dennis help yer sister. (*They go in.*) Bwoy how old are yu? Carrying on like yu six.

Pammy   I tink he still is.

Hope   So, yu still following my son around huh Pamela?

Pammy   I don' follow no one around.

Hope   Yu sleep wid im yet?

Pammy   Pardon?

Hope   Have you slept wid my son yet?

Pammy   Das none a yer business.

Hope   Juss hurry up, right, an' give im wat he wan', ca' if it money yu after . . .

Pammy   I don't wan' money.

Hope   . . . He nuh have none. It juss me and im fudda lookin' after im . . .

Pammy   Yu turn deaf?

Hope   Give wat im wan', and go.

Pammy   Yu don' know wat im wan'. Yu tink you do, yer spoil im rotten but yer don'.

Hope   My son nineteen years old. Wat yu tink is on de minds a bwoys im age? Yu go tell me I wrong now? It nuttin personal sweetheart.

Pammy   Yes it is. Everything yer say to me is personal. Ca' we both know if my name were anything but Simpson yu wouldn't be talkin' to me dis way. I here co' I wan' to be right.

Hope   Mout like yer tramp mudda.

Pammy   Comin' from yu das a compliment.

Hope   I juss counting de days when he finally get sick a yu.

Pammy   Dat won't happen.

Hope   It will, soon as yu open yer legs.

Pammy   Den I won't open my legs.

Hope   Yu be tellin' me yu virgin next Pamela.

Pammy   Yu not mekin' me upset again. How's Wally Mrs Gilbey? Yer nephew?

Hope   Me know who he is.

Pammy   I haven't seen im fer a while.

Hope   Yu know dam well yu, he and Dennis were by de bus station yesterday.

Pammy   Oh yes. We went Joey's bar. Wally love a drink yu know. Bwoy im can talk.

Hope   Listen right, my son don't wan' yu, he wan' dat! (*Points at* **Pammy**'*s crotch.*)

Hope *goes inside.* **Gravel** *enters the yard, whistling the same tune he did before. He is holding a brand new steering wheel.*

Gravel   Hey Pammy!

Pammy   Oh hi Mr Gilbey.

Gravel   Gravel! Me name Gravel chile, how many more times?

Pammy   Sorry.

Gravel   Hey, na, na, na, no long faces in dis yard, nossir! Now ware dat smile Pammy have, de one Gravel love? Ware it deh? Ware it deh?

Pammy *laughs.*

Gravel   Yes! Tank yu!

Gravel   Yer face could light up a room, Pammy Simpson.

Pammy   Yu aways say dat.

Gravel   Ca' it true, and Gravel aways speak de trut. Wat Hope bin sayin' to yu now?

Pammy   I don' care wat she say to me.

Gravel   It Dennis she should be yellin' at, not yu.

Pammy   She tell me dat he don't love me, he only after one ting. It not true is it?

Gravel   Course not chile, bwoy crazy 'bout yu. Im inside too? (**Pammy** *nods.*) Good!

Gravel *takes a secret swig from his flask.*

Gravel   Right! Gravel go work!

Pammy   Yu get it goin' yet? (**Gravel** *gets in the car and turns on the engine; it is still choking.*) Don' like dat.

Gravel   But it a start right. Gravel soon get her worried. Im tell her whom boss.

Pammy   I do love Dennis yu nuh Gravel. Im de only bwoy dat mek me laugh.

Gravel   Im mek me mad.

Pammy   But im aways goes on about wat im wan', never wat im have. Now he wan' be in dat flim.

Gravel   Yes. Stewart Granger, de hero.

Pammy   De fool. Man can' even act. Wid im long face.

Gravel   An' im big nose.

Pammy   An' im old, wid im grey hair. Dennis wan' be like dat?

Gravel   Dennis fool, Pammy. Im dream too much.

Pammy   Das wat im say about yu.

Gravel   Im can say wat im like. Hollywood! Superstar! Im and im mudda ferget, right? Gravel live in de white man world, im know wat it like, but deh nuh listen. Nossir. Gravel ever tell yu, im daddy was de best cab driver in Kingston? Quick time he get yu from A to B! Soon everybody talk 'bout me same way. Soon, Pammy. Deh all change de mind, Dennis too.

Pammy   Mek way we change it fer im den.

Gravel   How?

Pammy   When he come askin' fer a job, give it to im.

Gravel   Dennis go ask me?

Pammy   He promised.

Gravel   De only promise dat bwoy ever mek was never keep a promise.

Pammy   Dis time he promised his fiancée.

Gravel   Wat?

Pammy   Don't get upset.

Gravel   Fiancée?

Pammy   Dennis an' me juss wan'ed to keep it quiet fer a lickle while, we wan'ed to surprise yer both.

Gravel   Marriage, Pammy, to im! Yu sure 'bout dis?

Pammy   Yu juss say im mad about me.

Gravel   But im a bwoy dough Pammy.

Hope *comes out of the house, carrying a small bottle of pills and a glass of water.*

Hope   Gravel?

Gravel   Wat!

Hope   Come on.

Gravel   I look like a baby?

Hope   Don't act like one.

Gravel   Pammy, Gravel look sick to yu?

Pammy   Nossir!

Gravel   See, yu hear dat?

Hope   Juss come on.

Gravel *takes the pill and water. He burps. He and* **Pammy** *laugh.*

Hope   Yu drinkin' again? (**Gravel** *sucks his teeth.*) Fine. Yu juss carry on deh Gravel.

Gravel   Gravel busy.

Pammy   My mudda say deh's nuttin more nice dan seein' a man hard at work.

Gravel   Das right.

Hope   And man wid money.

Gravel   Awright Hope.

Pammy   I gone.

Gravel (*calls*)   Dennis!

Pammy   Na it awright.

Gravel   I'll get im chile, Dennis!

Pammy   Tell im I see im later.

Hope   Let her go Gravel. She muss have friends to meet, right Pamela?

Pammy   Right. How's yer nephew Wally, Gravel?

Gravel   Im fine.

Pammy   Tell im I say hello right . . . I gone (*Exit.*)

Gravel *gives* **Hope** *a look.*

Hope   Wat? Look Gravel dat sweet gyal act nuh fool me right.

Gravel   Pammy not like her mudda.

Hope   Whu yu aways believe her?

Gravel   Ca' Pammy nuh lie. Why she ask after Walford when she see im all de time?

Hope   Me dunno. Who know wat go on in de gyal head?

Dennis *comes into the yard. He has* **Little Hope** *on his shoulders.*

Dennis (*announces*)   Tonight's menu. Lickle Hope soup!

Little Hope   No!

Dennis   Yes!

Gravel   Put yer sister down and come over here.

Little Hope   Don't shout at im.

Hope   Inside, Lickle Hope.

Little Hope *runs back in.*

Gravel   Wat dis marriage business wid yu and Pammy?

Hope   Wat!

Dennis   I not go marry Pammy, Mama.

Gravel   Not wat she tink.

Dennis   I know.

Gravel   So wat yu go do?

Dennis   I don't know.

Gravel   Well yu better find out.

Dennis   Look, I like de girl Pops, but she wan' marry me. She mekin' all kind a plans. I try tell her, but she nuh listen.

Gravel   Bwoy don't play wid me.

Dennis   I not playin' wid yu Pops.

Gravel   Yer playin' wid me.

Dennis   Yu wan' me to marry her den?

Gravel   Wid wat, yu have no money.

Dennis   I know dat.

Gravel   Yu have no job.

Dennis   I know dat too.

Gravel   Lord knows wat a nice gyal like dat see in yu. She deserve better.

Hope   A Simpson.

Gravel   She a human being, Hope.

Hope   Oh yes?

Gravel   An' deh feel, deh hurt. Yu hearin' me Dennis?

Dennis   Is whole street can hear yu.

Gravel   Are yu hearin' me!

Dennis   Why yu aways have to look at me wid dat long face a yours? It kill yu to smile? Try it it easy, yu juss move yer mout like so . . .

Gravel   Don' joke wid me Dennis. Gravel tell yu awready im don' like it. Yu tell dat gyal how yu really feel right, or Gravel will.

Dennis   Fine.

Gravel   Well?

Dennis   Yu wan' me to go now?

Gravel   Right now.

Dennis   I gone.

Gravel   She also say yu wan' to help me wid de cab. Dat a lie too?

Dennis   Yu tell me.

Gravel   Don't matter, ca' yu workin' wid me.

Dennis   Come on Pops, wat I know about cars?

Gravel   Gravel teach yu.

Dennis   An' wat yu know?

Gravel   Everyting my Daddy teach me.

Dennis   Mama?

Hope   Don't look at me son.

Gravel   Yu wan' stop tinkin' wid dat. (*Points to his own crotch.*)

Dennis   Tanks but I got my own ting.

Gravel   Every ting a nasty joke to yu.

Dennis   Least me know how to joke. An' yu mad if yer tink I go waste my life drivin' cab.

Gravel   Yer wan' live in my house? Eat my food? From now on yu stay ware Gravel keep im eye on yu, no more tiefing, no more watchin' dat fool Stewart Granger.

Hope   Stewart Granger no fool.

Gravel (*sees* **Dennis** *is still there*)   Yu still here?

Dennis   Yu still talkin'.

Gravel   Go see Pammy.

Dennis   I will if yu let me.

Gravel   Gravel not stoppin' yu.

Dennis   Yu still talkin' to me.

Gravel I am not.

Dennis Yu are Pops.

Gravel I am not . . .

Dennis Yer are . . .

Hope Dennis, juss go.

Dennis *exits*.

Gravel I suppose yu tink Gravel doing de wrong ting again?

Hope Me nuh say a word.

Gravel Yu encourage im.

Hope I do not.

Gravel Fillin' up im head, tellin' im he can do wat he wan'.

Hope Im can do wat im wan'. Im can do any ting, yu don' know yer own son by now? And Dennis wouldn't be de way he was wid dat gyal, if gyals like dat didn't lie down on deh back. Dat Pammy Simpson, she have yu fooled.

Gravel Nobody have Gravel fooled.

Hope Oh, an' I suppose Ned Williams isn't laughing behind yer back right now?

Gravel No an' yer know why? Ca' only dis mornin' right, im offer to buy de car back: twice more dan wat Gravel pay.

Hope And yu say no.

Gravel Of course me say no. Ned worried, im know Gravel can do it, he probably bin tinking about starting up a cab business imself.

Hope Well it better work dis time. Ca' me sewing dresses is not enough to feed us all. (*Puts her arm round him.*) Gravel.

Gravel Wat yu doin'?

Hope   Oh shush man.

Gravel   Gravel wan' work, Hope.

Hope   Car not going any place. Yu allowed to hold me as well yer nuh, Gravel.

Gravel *feels awkward with this show of emotion from* **Hope**. *He is unsure what to do.*

Hope   I know wat yu tinkin'.

Gravel   Do yu?

Hope   Im a young man now.

Gravel   Das wat frighten me.

Hope   He wan' to live im own life.

Gravel   Don't mean he have to hurt dat girl right! He don' have to hurt anybody.

Hope   Why yu angry wid me?

Gravel   Gravel not angry.

Hope   Yu aways angry. Why yu ever get angry wid dem?

Gravel   Gravel don' care . . .

Hope   . . . wat dem tink. Well im should. Ca' it me, yer son and yer daughter, de ones dat have to stand up to dem. Yu tink any one a dem care about yu de way we do?

Gravel   I don' wan' yu to care.

Hope   Wat den?

Gravel *holds his wife. He kisses her.*

Hope   Awright man, juss go easy yeah?

Gravel *pulls away from her.*

Hope   All me say . . .

Gravel   Yu tink Gravel weak, Gravel not weak right, Gravel strong, Gravel strong right, im strong.

Gravel *runs round the yard.*

Hope   Gravel stop it, stop it man!

Gravel   Gravel strong.

Hope   Awright enough yeah? Stop it.

Gravel *gets on the ground and does sit-ups.*

Hope (*pleading*)   Gravel!

Gravel *pushes* **Hope** *away as she tries to stop him.*

Hope   For God's sake nuh man. Wa wrong wid yu?

Gravel   Gravel strong, Gravel strong, Gravel strong . . .

Hope   Yu wan' kill yerself? Yu wan' kill yerself Gravel, well go ahead! (*Goes back in the house.*)

Gravel   Gravel strong, Gravel strong, Gravel . . . (*Breaks down in tears.*)

Scene Three

Next day in the yard. **Dennis** *and* **Wally** *are sitting on top of the car watching the film being made.* **Wally** *has the binoculars.*

Wally (*turned on*)   Man who is dat woman? She look nice. I wonder if dis movie an X we might see her tittie or summin. Yu ever see a white woman's tittie?

Dennis   Nearly.

Wally   Is wat yu mean 'nearly'?

Dennis   When I was lickle Mama took me to see *Dr No*, James Bond and im gal, Honey Ryder, dem get caught an' deh have to go through a shower ca' de get radiation, an' fer lickle second right, yu can see bit a de gal tittie. Nice.

Wally   Real life Dennis, not de movies.

Dennis   It was real life. Dat was her real tittie I saw, I don't think we were supposed to see it, musta bin a mistake deh mek . . .

Wally   Awright, have yu ever see a white woman tittie outside de cinema?

Dennis   No.

Wally   Tank you. *Dr No*! Yu carry on like yer pops sumtimes.

Dennis   Yer ever see a white woman tittie den?

Wally   Last summer when I was working in de hotel. I had to bring a drink to sum white woman lying on de beach. She lift up her head right, an' her bikini top drop down, boom, me see dem! She look nice too. And yer know wat, she smile at me. She tell me to go jump her right deh.

Dennis   Lie.

Wally   It trut. Dem white women love de black man. Deh feel no shame, too. Broad daylight me have her!

Dennis   Yu lie man.

Wally   Well wat yu know, bwoy! Yu nuh even grind yer gal yet. If dat were me right, me woulda had her from time! Wa' wrong wid yu? She a Simpson gyal Dennis, she easy, she ripe. If yer can't grind dat yu be a batayman.

Dennis   How yu know me nuh grind her awready?

Wally   Ca' yu woulda said. Ca' I can aways tell when yu lie. Yu grind her Dennis, have yu, have yu? Have yu, have yu . . .

Dennis   No! I wan' grind her so bad, my ting get hard, it feel like it go brok off.

Wally   Batayman!

Dennis   Maybe I should marry her.

Wally   Yer mad! Listen right, marriage ain't nuttin but a bad word. Yu see me, no woman go trap me.

Dennis   Wat 'bout dat married woman yu messin' wid? I see de way yu look when yu chat 'bout her.

Wally   Me nuh love her. Only oder day right, she beg me to tek her round corner. I said to her 'Na woman. Wally got tings to do, people to see', but she on her hands and knees. So I did, keep her quiet yer know. She stuck on me man, way Wally like it.

Dennis   Min' her husband.

Wally   Man a jack arse. Fool don't deserve woman like dat.

Dennis   See? Yu love her man.

Wally   Shut up man, cha yer wan' to marry Pammy go ahead. I bored. Let's go to de bus station.

Dennis   Hold on. Deh look, deh's Granger. I wish Mama was here.

Wally   Come on man.

Dennis   Wait.

Dennis *sees something. He laughs out.*

Wally (*takes the binoculars*)   Nuh man!

Dennis   Gw'n Granger.

Wally   If dat were real life, no way could a old man like dat beat up six young man. See dat bwoy over deh, holdin' Granger by de neck? Who im look like to yu?

Dennis   Manny Christie! How de hell he get a part in de flim? He can't act.

Wally   Im don't need to act, juss fight.

Dennis (*yelling*)   Yu ugly wretch Manny!

Wally   Im getting eighty dollars to be ugly.

Dennis   Come on Granger, tump im!

Wally   Bus station?

Dennis   Hold on a minute. Manny lying on de floor now, summin happened. Look like he broke im leg or summin.

Wally   Obeah man!

Dennis   Watch me now.

Wally   Deh fling you out awready.

Dennis   I juss go stand near. I de same shape as Manny, deh soon spot me.

Wally   Yer askin' fer trouble Dennis.

Dennis   I go come back a star Wally! Watch me now . . .

Dennis *loses his balance and falls off the car.* **Wally** *laughs out loud.*

Act Two

Scene One

Back yard. A week later. **Hope** *is sitting down sewing a dress.*
Gravel *is in the car. He turns on the engine. It is still choking.*
Hope *looks at him.*

Gravel   Wat? (*Goes inside.*)

Dennis *bursts into the yard. He is dressed in a very smart expensive
new suit. He strolls in singing along to the James Bond theme tune.*

Dennis (*in a Sean Connery accent*)   You are looking very
delicious tonight, Miss Moneypenny.

Hope   Not a brass farding.

Dennis   Money! Dear mother I do not require money.

Hope (*amazed*)   Oh my Lord! Is dis my son?

Dennis   Smart, right?

Hope   How much it cost?

Dennis   Enough. Yer shoulda seen me walk right into dat
shop, put me money down, and say, me wan' dat suit,
gimme it! (*Sniffs.*) I love de smell a a new suit.

Hope (*sniffing the suit as well*)   Dennis man, yu smell good!

Dennis   Told yu I'd come back a star Mama.

Hope   De give yu more to do in de flim?

Dennis   Yes, no more crowd scenes fer me. De director
pick me out imself to start up a bar fight wid Granger.

Hope   Yu start up a bar fight wid Granger?

Dennis   Yeah man.

Hope   So wat happen?

Dennis   I fling a bokkle at Granger's head, he hit me wid im chair, next ting whole bar break out in a fight. After dat right, de director come over, im tap me on de shoulder and im say, 'Well done'.

Hope (*so proud*)   Oh Dennis!

Dennis   Close yer eyes Mama.

Hope   Why?

Dennis   Juss close dem.

Hope   Lord Jesus, why yu love to tease me so?

Dennis *disappears through the yard door, he comes back a second later, holding an A4 size photograph.*

Dennis   Keep dem closed.

Hope   Dem closed.

Dennis   Now hold out yer hands.

Hope   Wat yu got fer me?

Dennis *places the photograph on her hands.*

Dennis   Open!

Hope *opens her eyes. She sees what* **Dennis** *has given her.*

Hope   But Jesus Christ!

Dennis   Tell yu I get yu it.

Hope (*reading*)   'To Hope Gilbey, my No.1 fan. Love and best wishes from Stewart Granger.' (*Thrilled.*) Thank yu. Oh my . . . how de hell yu get dis?

Dennis   I ask im fer it.

Hope   Yu say yu can hardly get near im, when yer get near im?

Dennis   It happen by accident. I was juss walking along, tekin' a break, an' I juss see im, sitting in im own chair, reading im paper – alone dis time. He aways before had big hefty people watchin' over im, movin' us away from im. So I juss tell myself, 'Do it Dennis'. I tek a deep breath, walk straight over to im . . .

Hope (*eager*)   Yes?

Dennis   I said, Wa' appenin'? I'm Dennis Gilbey.

Hope   Wa' appenin'?

Dennis   Yeah.

Hope   Yu say 'wa' appenin'' to Stewart Granger? Im a Hollywood superstar Dennis, he come from Englan'. You know how posh dem talk, yu can't say tings like 'wa' appening' to im.

Dennis   Mama he didn't mind, im nice.

Hope   So wat im say?

Dennis (*putting on a posh English accent*)   'How do you do?'

Hope (*dreamy*)   'How do you do.' Wat else?

Dennis   He tought I was really good beating im up an' dat, so I says, 'Well I tink yer really good too, Mr Granger, pretendin' yer young when yu really old.'

Hope   Yu didn't? Dennis!

Dennis   Im laugh. He is old now though Mama, I see im face real close, im have a whole heap a wrinkles.

Hope   Im aways be young to me. Wat else?

Dennis   Das it. His people come back and pushed me away from im, but not before I got yu dat, an' told im all about yu. How yu seen all im flims since when yu were lickle, how yu tek me to see dem.

Hope (*thrilled*)   He ask yu wat my favourite one was?

Dennis   *Prisoner of Zenda*!

Dennis *grabs one of his father's spanners. He waves it about, pretending it is a sword.*

Dennis Deh going back to England soon, finish de movie. Yu know wat, maybe he might speak to de director and get me a bigger part in de flim. Deh might tek me back to England wid dem. Granger like me Mama.

Hope Course im like yu, why shouldn't he like yu? Yu is a good actor bwoy.

Dennis Can't wait to see de look on Pammy's face.

Hope I tought yu tell de gyal to clear off.

Dennis Not yet. Soon Mama.

Hope I know all about yer soons. Deh don' come till next year. Yu got more important tings to do now than go chasin' after dat slut.

Dennis I tell her.

Hope Yu better.

Dennis I will. Yu like yer present?

Hope Course me like it. (*Admires her picture.*) I go have to buy a nice frame fer dis man, put it up in de living room. (*In love.*) Stewart Granger!

Dennis How old was Stewart Granger when im mek *King Solomon's Mines*?

Hope Thirty-six.

Dennis Wat year it come out?

Hope 1949.

Dennis Who win Best Actor Oscar in 1956?

Hope Yul Brynner.

Dennis Wat flim?

Hope *King an' I.*

Dennis Who starred wid Humphrey Bogart in *Sabrina Fair*?

Hope   William Holden, Audrey Hepburn.

Dennis   Wat year Dennis Gilbey win im first Oscar? What year im marry Natalie Wood?

Hope   Oh so it she now?

Dennis   When I rich and famous, how many house yu wan'?

Hope   Just de one darling.

Dennis   I buy Lickle Hope a boat, and twenty-odd cars fer Pops to fix up.

Hope   We'll hardly see im den. Buy im a hundred.

Dennis   How come yu never tek im to see a Stewart Granger flim Mama?

Hope   Gravel more a a Gary Cooper man. Me an' yer Uncle Neville de ones who love Granger. Every time a new flim come, we first in de queue. Going to de movies wid im was fun man.

Dennis   Maybe yu shoulda married im den. Yu is a good looking woman yer nuh, Mama.

Hope   Tank yu kind sir.

Dennis   Musta had plenty men running after yu.

Hope   Dennis Gilbey wat yu trying to say?

Dennis   Why yu choose Pops?

Hope   Don't speak about yer fudda so, Dennis.

Dennis   All yer life yu wan' to sew dress?

Hope   Im a wonderful man.

Dennis   Wat im ever done tha' bin wonderful?

Hope   He left England to be wid me.

Dennis   But he shoulda married you deh. I wouda bin born deh. Imagine de kinda life we coulda had.

Hope   Yu know how old yer fudda was when I first met im? Eleven. I musta bin 'bout seven. Guess wat im doing? Tap dancin' outside Joey's bar fer money. He was good. Everybody watchin' dis lickle country bwoy wid im fancy steps. He mek good money, but nobody watchin' im lickle friend Bernie tekin' deh wallet and money outta all deh pockets.

Dennis (*laughs*)   Gravel Gilbey!

Hope   Yes.

Dennis   Scam fer money?

Hope   When I saw dat man, I knew dat was a bwoy I could have fun with.

Dennis   So wat happened to im den?

Hope   Nuttin.

Dennis   Oh come on.

Hope   Im still dat bwoy Dennis, yu juss mus look fer it.

Gravel *comes out.*

Dennis   Hey Pops!

Dennis *tries to tap dance, he extends his hand to* **Gravel**, *inviting him to join in.*

Gravel (*unimpressed*)   Yu fall sumware on yer head?

Dennis   No.

Gravel (*takes the spanner off* **Dennis**)   Dis look like toy to yu?

Dennis   Like my suit Pops?

Gravel   Ware yu tief it? I hope yu givin' yer mudda money.

Dennis (*taking out a wad of notes, gives* **Hope** *some*)   Here you are Mother, buy yourself something ever so nice out a that.

Gravel   Oh yes we de big man now don't it.

Dennis   An' yu hate dat don't it?

Gravel   Tell me summin. Wat yu go do when de flim finish? Tiefin'? Ca' if yu are, let me tell yu summin right . . .

Dennis   I don't tief no more.

Gravel   So wat yu go do?

Dennis   If yu mus know, I go to Englan', I go act.

Gravel   Yu go England? (*Laughs.*) Yu wouldn't last two days.

Dennis   Yu lasted two years.

Gravel   Juss ca' deh give yu a lickle bit a money to farm de fool Dennis . . .

Dennis   I not farmin' de fool! Come on Pops, yer son get beaten up by Stewart Granger.

Gravel   Old man like im.

Hope   Im not dat old.

Gravel   Im old.

Dennis   It an important scene, de man playing my boss has kidnapped Granger's wife, so he come out here to rescue her, but den she and de man . . .

Gravel   Gravel don't wan' to hear none a yer stupidness . . .

Dennis   Why yu love to put me down?

Gravel   . . . me done!

Dennis   If I go Mama, I go live in London. Dass ware Granger was born? Tell me about London, Pops.

Gravel   It a dirty nasty place.

Hope   London is very nice.

Gravel   How would yu know?

Hope   It aways look nice when deh show it in a flim.

Gravel   Wat is my wife talking about?

Hope   Las one I see, dis couple walk by de river – wat it called? Thames – de moon was out, it was night, it look so romantic.

Gravel (*mimicking*)   Oh it were so romantic! Who was in de movie, let me guess, Stewart-blasted-Granger? Batayman.

Dennis   Wat?

Hope   Stewart Granger no batayman!

Gravel   Im a batayman.

Hope   Im have a whole heap a woman.

Gravel   Men too. Im and Cary Grant having a lickle ting.

Dennis (*shocked*)   Cary Grant!

Hope   Juss ignore im Dennis.

Dennis   Cary Grant!

Hope   Dennis!

Dennis   I don't know now Mama, I not so sure now.

Hope   Das not yu said a minute ago.

Dennis   But why be all friendly to a bwoy im hardly know?

Hope   Ca' im a nice man, like yu say. Don't be so stupid.

Dennis   I not stupid! Pops, yer wrong.

Gravel   Awright. But when yu drop yer hat, kick it home.

Dennis (*he gets it*)   Hey!

Hope   Bwoy shut up. (*To* **Gravel**.) Is ware yu hear all dis?

Gravel   Yu be surprised wat Gravel hear on de streets a London. It a sinful place, Gravel keep telling yu. Yu wanna know wat it like Dennis? One time me an' yer Uncle Neville get a job working in sum bar in London. It seem awright, till we see two men coming in holding hands, kissing! Gravel ask Neville, wat kinda club is dis?

Hope   Places like dat exist all over Gravel.

Gravel   Not here deh don't.

Hope   Oh no? Yer wan' tek look down Harbor Street, de two a yu.

Dennis   Na das awright.

Gravel   Gravel not finished.

Hope   So finish.

Gravel   Next ting we know, police come kicking down de door, everyone run like rat, who get catch?

Dennis   Yu an' Uncle Neville?

Gravel   Im gone, run off. He aways did dat. Leaving me to clear up im mess.

Dennis   It'll never happen to me man.

Gravel   Oh yu tink so?

Dennis   I not like yu Pops, when trouble come, me run.

Gravel   Yu don' tink I tried?

Dennis   Not hard enough.

Gravel   Deh arrested me.

Dennis   But not Uncle Neville, ca' im smart. Shoulda tumped dem in de head and run. It wat me woulda done.

Gravel   How?

Dennis   Wat?

Gravel   How? Show me how bwoy.

Hope Gravel?

Gravel Gravel wat! I wan' me son to show me. Show me bwoy. Yu afraid?

Dennis *holds up his fists.*

Gravel Now, come an' hit me. Wat yu laughin' fer?

Dennis I don't wan' hit yu Pops.

Gravel Prove I raise no weak bwoy.

Hope Tek it easy please.

Gravel (*brushing her away*) Don't do yer daddy no favours now, right?

Hope Stop dis.

Gravel Come on!

Dennis *does not want to do this. He clips* **Gravel** *on the cheek.*

Gravel Gravel say hit not tickle.

Dennis *goes to hit him but* **Gravel** *dodges around him a few times.*

Gravel Yu not hitting me bwoy.

Hope Slow down.

Gravel Yer daddy too quick fer yu?

Dennis No.

Gravel Yu lie!

Dennis I don't wan' to hit yu pops.

Gravel (*shoving him hard*) Yu tink yu better than me right? Is dat wat yu tink!

Hope Come on . . .

Gravel Is dat wat yu tink Dennis?

Dennis It wat I know.

Gravel *throws a punch of his own, striking* **Dennis** *in the face.*

Hope   Gravel!

Gravel   See it deh! Like lightning.

Hope   Let me see . . .

Dennis   I'm fine! (*Leaves the yard.*)

Hope   Why?

Gravel   Im not goin' to Englan', Hope.

Hope   Das up to im man.

Gravel   Im not goin' all dat way to follow im daddy right. Im not followin' Neville.

Hope   Gravel, yu is im fudda.

Gravel   He got too much a im Daddy in im.

Hope   Don' say dat.

Gravel   He even had to grow up wid de same face.

Hope   So wat man? It don' matter. It doesn't matter Gravel. It yu who raise im. Yu is im fudda. Yu can't keep blamin' Neville fer all dis.

Gravel   Gravel blaming yu. From de day de bwoy could talk, yer tekin' im to see flim.

Hope   And so?

Gravel   So how many times I watch yu riding off on de back a Neville's bike to see flim? How many times?

Hope   Yu nuh see de man in twenty years, and yer still jealous a im.

Gravel   Ca' yu mek me see im!

Hope   How? How am I doing dat?

Gravel   Sonny Blake.

Hope   God's sake nuh man.

Gravel   Joe Newman.

Hope   Ancient history, Gravel.

Gravel   Walford! 'Bout ancient history.

Hope   Gravel . . .

Gravel   Yer own nephew, my sister's child. Yu is dirty nasty woman. Don't tell me I nuh see my broder in twenty years right, nuh tell me dat. Ca' yu still wan' im.

Hope   I married yu. I love yu.

Gravel   But yu still wan' im. Yu wan' im Hope. Tell me say yu wan' im, tell me say yu wan' im, tell me yu say yu want him Hope . . .

Hope   Gravel . . .

Gravel   Tell me say yu wan' im.

Hope   Stop it.

Gravel   Tell me.

Hope   Awright I wan' im! I wan' im to mek love to me like he used to on de beach, I wan' to feel im hands strokin' my thigh, I wanna feel my hands touchin' im chest, im face, I wan' feel love dat mek me live a whole lifetime's-worth in one night! Yu happy now, is dat wat yu wan' fer me to say to yu?

Gravel   Awright den, Gravel tired right. First ting tomorrow, I go draw out my money from de bank and give yu.

Hope   Wat yu chat 'bout now?

Gravel   Yu go Englan'. No more talk or dreamin' right? Yu go find im.

Hope   I go Englan', and who go tek care a yu?

Gravel   I DON'T NEED NOBODY TO TEK CARE A ME!

Gravel *holds his chest.*

Hope   Gravel? Oh my Lord no Gravel, come, come Gravel, come. Don't fight me, come on.

Hope *takes* **Gravel** *inside.*

In the street. **Pammy** *is nursing* **Dennis***'s bleeding face.*

Dennis   I shoulda knock im head right off!

Pammy   Yu can't do dat.

Dennis   He nearly do it to me.

Pammy   Wat yu do to mek im angry?

Dennis   Yeah gw'n, tek im side like yer aways do. Dis is de way im is Pammy, I keep telling but yer nuh believe me. He can't stand de fact that I better than im. And I am. No one laugh at me. Yu hear any one call me Midas? Yu know how many times I had to fight oder bwoys at school who were calling im names? An' were im grateful? (*Mimics.*) 'Gravel don't need yu fighting my battles!' Now it Lickle Hope's turn to fight, I feel sorry fer her. I ain't letting my pikne go through dat. Gonna give dem wat de wan', deh dreams go come true. Can I stay wid yu tonight?

Pammy   Dennis.

Dennis   I won't mek noise. Come on Pammy, please.

Pammy   Yu can sleep on de floor.

Dennis   Floor bad fer my back. Can't I share de bed wid yu? I nuh snore. (**Pammy** *hits him.*) Pammy!

Pammy   Move from me before I mek yer whole body bleed.

Dennis   All me say man . . .

Pammy   I know wat yu said. Got it all planned right? Come over here fer a lickle sympathy den get me into bed.

Dennis   No Pammy.

Pammy   Yes Dennis!

Dennis   Look I had a bad day yer nuh . . .

Pammy   And I haven't? It aways about yu Dennis. Yu an' yer pops fighting again, yu and yer stupid flim, running from Lester. Yu ever stop to tink about me? Yu ever ask 'How was yer day Pammy?'

Dennis   How was yer day Pammy?

Pammy   Awful.

Dennis   Why wat happen?

Pammy   Wass de point, yu don't care. Yu juss wan' tek me to bed so yer can tell Wally an' all yer friends.

Dennis   Wat happen?

Pammy   Mama had to throw sum man out ca' im getting too rough wid her. He wan'ed her to do all kind a nasty tings. Next ting I know im following me to de shop, he grabbed me from behind, sayin' in my ear if my mama won't do it, he go mek me do it. I kick im so hard and run.

Dennis   De nasty sunafabitch! Who was it? Tell me who it was, Pammy, I break im neck.

Pammy   I don't wan' yu breakin' anyone's neck.

Dennis   Pammy, no one does dat to yu an' lives right? Yu hearing me?

Pammy   I wan' yu to understand, understand me.

Dennis   I do understand yu.

Pammy   De only reason that man come after me Dennis ca' he tinks I juss like me mudda. Everyone tinks I like me mudda. I can't give yu wat yer wan' – not till I sure.

Dennis   Feel my heart, Pammy. Feel it.

Pammy (*with her hand on his chest*)   It like a drum gone mad.

Dennis   It goes like dat, every time I wid yu. Everytime I see yu. Yu everyting to me, yer de only ting on dis island worth staying fer, Pammy Simpson.

Pammy   Am I?

Dennis   Wat more me have to do to prove it? (*Kisses her, unbuttons her blouse.*)

Pammy   Don't ever hurt me Dennis.

Scene Two

Weeks later. **Hope** *is in her usual spot, on top of the car, watching the film with the binoculars.*

Hope   Gw'n Granger, teach dem sum manners.

Wally *enters the yard, he squeezes her behind.*

Hope   Walford!

Wally   Sorry Auntie.

Hope   Wat yu wan'?

Wally   Suck on yer tittie till me eye pop out. Dem still filmin'?

Hope   Shush.

Wally   Dem can't hear.

Wally *tries to distract* **Hope**'s *attention by running his hand up and down her leg.*

Hope   Stop it.

Wally   No one here.

Hope   I don't care. I wan' watch dis awright?

Wally   Come on.

Hope   Yu got three minutes.

Wally   Wat?

Hope   Dem reloading de camera, it aways tek dem 'bout three minutes.

Wally   Wat yu expect me to do in three minutes?

Hope   Tell me wat yu wan'.

Wally   Guess!

Hope (*slaps his hand away*)   No!

Wally   Dis woman drive me mad!

Hope   Yu nuh even ask how yer uncle doing.

Wally (*uninterested*)   How Uncle Gravel doing?

Hope   He coulda dead yu nuh Walford?

Wally   Awright, so how im doing?

Hope   Im fine, im tekin' it easy now.

Wally   Good, now come home wid me.

Hope   I watchin' de flim.

Wally   But me ting get big. Yu wan' me to show yu? Hope? Wat me do?

Hope   Who yu bin talkin' to Wally?

Wally   Nobody.

Hope   So how come Pammy and Gravel know?

Wally   Deh know?

Hope   How come deh know? Yu shooting off yer mout, tellin' how yer bin grinding a married woman? Is that how deh hear? So how come deh know den?

Wally   Deh musta guess.

Hope   Wat yu bin sayin' to mek dem guess?

Wally   Nuttin! Look, look I don't even care, right? Pammy won't say anyting, Gravel nuttin but a jackass and im sick, wat can he do?

Hope   Don't yu dare talk about my husband so.

Wally   We be more careful.

Hope   No Walford. No more.

Wally   Yu mad.

Hope   It not up to yu.

Wally   I is no door yu can juss open and shut yu nuh.

Hope   Yu tink I go let yu mek fool a me?

Wally   Me sorry.

Hope   Don' beg.

Wally   Me nuh beg.

Hope   Yer three minutes up.

Wally   Is wat yer wan' from me den? Yer wan' fer me to carry sword, kill whole heap a men, jump through window like Stewart Granger? Mek women dead fer me? Is dat de kinda man yer wan'?

Hope   At least he can never hurt me.

Wally   I wan' love yu.

Hope   Yu wan' fuck me!

Wally   Me love yu.

Hope   Wally yu is juss a bwoy. Gw'n awright, lemme.

Wally   Yu wan' half a Kingston to know 'bout us, oder half laughin' at Uncle Gravel?

Hope   An' de rest to watch yer mama throw yer arse out, right before yer fudda knock off yer stupid lickle head! And yu know he will. Yu lickle fool.

Wally   Too bad Dennis got a mama like yu, all it tek fer sumone to open im mouth, an' boom, he know de trut. He might wan' to do summin stupid, come after me. Last ting I wan', fer me to hurt me cousin Auntie.

Hope   Stay away from my son. Im worth ten a yu.

Wally   Im a bwoy too.

Hope   Im special.

Wally   So special he mek Pammy pregnant?

Hope   Wat?

Wally   Her mudda tell me de oder day. I sorry. Look at me. Juss tell me wat yu wan' Hope . . .

Hope   Get out, get out.

Wally   Yu don't wan' my ting? Nuff gyals wan' my ting!

Wally *leaves.* **Hope** *goes back into the house.*

Little Hope *and* **Dennis** *come running into the yard shortly afterwards, shooting at each other with their fingers as guns. They play around all over the yard until* **Dennis** *clutches his heart and drops down dead.* **Little Hope** *continues to shoot at him while he's down. She eventually stops.*

Little Hope   Dennis?

Dennis   Yeah?

Little Hope   Yu dead?

Dennis   Mash up.

They both laugh as they tickle each other.

Gravel (*coming out*)   Yu plannin' on lying on de ground all day?

Little Hope   Daddy!

Little Hope *runs over to give her father a hug.*

Gravel   Easy chile yer wan' give me more pain?

Little Hope   Yu supposed to be resting in bed.

Gravel   Oh yu my nurse now?

Little Hope   Yes!

Gravel   No, yu is me pride!

Little Hope   We got a surprise fer yu Daddy, show im Dennis, show im.

Dennis *turns on the engine. It is running smoothly.*

Gravel   Wat de hell?

Little Hope   Dennis bin working on it all week Daddy.

Gravel   How?

Dennis   Few hours, mostly at night.

Gravel   No. (*Points to the car.*) How?

Dennis   Engine older than yu Pops, but she like me.

Little Hope   I helped as well Daddy. I tink yu should call de business Gravel & Son & Daughter. Wait!

Little Hope *heads for the house.*

Gravel   Ware yu goin'?

Gravel and **Dennis** *remain silent, neither sure what to say to the other.* **Little Hope** *returns with a camera.*

Little Hope   Put yer arm round im Daddy, come on.

Gravel and **Dennis** *pose nervously as* **Little Hope** *takes their picture. She runs to the fence and starts climbing.*

Gravel   Chile why yu nuh use de door? Ware yu going?

Little Hope   Tell me friends no one laughs at my pops no more. (*Exit.*)

Gravel   Yu ever see dat chile keep still?

Dennis   Nope. Yu had me scared yu nuh Pops.

Gravel   Is dat why yu do it, ca' yu wan' favour?

Dennis   No.

Gravel   Nuttin changed right.

Dennis   Right.

Gravel   Yu still too rude.

Dennis   Yep.

Gravel *turns the engine on again. He loves the sound of what he is hearing but tries not to show it.*

Gravel   Why yu watch me fer? Shouldn't yu be off actin'?

Dennis   Later. I bin counting all de things deh got me doing, I going to be in five different scenes yer nuh Pops, five.

Gravel *takes out his flask.* **Dennis** *takes the flask off him.*

Gravel   Gimme back me flask!

Dennis   Yu know ware dis drink going?

Gravel   Down my throat, gimme!

Dennis *pours the drink on to the ground.*

Gravel   Yu see de problem wid yu is right, yu never had enough licks as a child.

Dennis   Ca' me too fast fer yu.

Gravel   Ca' yu aways hide behind yer mudda. 'Mummy, Mummy, Daddy wan' hit me!' She never use belt on yer tail once.

Dennis   Yeah, give de child sum licks.

Gravel   Wat else is deh?

Dennis   Talkin'? Find out why de child do wat im do.

Gravel   Child do wat im do ca' im too renk. Nuttin wrong wid licks, when fuddas tell deh pikne to do summin, deh do it, or deh get licks. Don't mean yu don' love dem.

Dennis   Yu nuh feel de child need to hear it?

Gravel   Is which flim yu hear dat? I keep tellin' yu dem Hollywood people don't know nuttin 'bout life.

Dennis   Well yu'll be pleased to know deh nearly finish.

Gravel   Good.

Dennis   Deh all be going home.

Gravel   Good.

Dennis   I go to Englan' Pops.

Gravel   When?

Dennis   Soon. I got my money save. I showed Granger my speech from Romeo an' Juliet, he say I should audition for dat school RADA. I go soon.

Gravel   Yu juss go jump on a boat, show yer speech to dem people an' boom! Deh let yu in? (*Laughs.*)

Dennis   Why is dat so hard fer yu?

Gravel   Yu don't know nuttin 'bout wat out deh Dennis.

Dennis   Tell me den.

Gravel   Yu only wan' wat yu wan' to hear.

Dennis   I wanna hear yu.

Gravel   Awright. Gravel leave im home ca' he wan' see de rest a de world.

Dennis   Yeah?

Gravel   Gravel see de world fer wat it is, nasty dirty place . . .

Dennis   Pops?

Gravel . . . so he come back to im home, ware im belong.

Dennis Das not . . .

Gravel . . . not wat yu wan' to hear? Yu see wat I mean?

Dennis Wat about Uncle Neville den?

Gravel Wat dis have to do wid im?

Dennis Im still deh.

Gravel Wid im white woman, wid my money im tief!

Dennis Don't mean it go happen to me. I not like yu. I could be de first Jamaican ever to win Oscar. De first!

Gravel Das yer mudda talkin' bwoy. I suppose she tell yu to go.

Dennis She tell me I should do wass right fer me.

Gravel And wat about Pammy? Yer fiancée, in case yu ferget.

Dennis She'll find sumone else. Sumone better right?

Gravel Yu could do a whole lot worse than her yu know son. She a lovely gyal Dennis.

Dennis I know dat. But I have to do dis. Don't go on awright.

Gravel Juss tell me summin right . . .

Dennis No!

Gravel All dem flims yer mama tek yu to see, yu ever see one wid a black man in de lead?

Dennis No.

Gravel See dat James Bond flim Dr watimname . . .

Dennis *Dr No*.

Gravel Right. James Bond im have a friend?

Dennis Quarrel?

Gravel   Quarrel! Now im smart right, good wid a knife, drive a boat, everyting. So how come it im who have de carry de man shoes, who get kill by dat dragon ting?

Dennis   Ca' im save Bond life.

Gravel   Why?

Dennis   Ca' Bond de hero.

Gravel   Why?

Dennis   Ca' im James Bond, Pops!

Gravel   Why? Why couldn't Bond be de one dat get dead up and . . .

Dennis   Yu can't kill James Bond.

Gravel   . . . Quarrel have de gyal? Gravel know why. It wat white people wan' it, it way it go stay. Deh don' wan' us deh.

Dennis   But I can change tings Pops, I wan' to try, is why yu never listen . . .

Gravel   De Alamo, Johnny Wayne! Juss before de Mexicans come and kill up everybody, Johnny Wayne let im slave go, tell im he a free man. So wat de fool go an' do, decide to stay so he can get kill up wid everyone else. If dat were me right, Gravel would be sayin' to Johnny Wayne 'Me gone. It my black arse me a look out fer'.

Dennis   Richard Widmark.

Gravel   Wat yu say?

Dennis   Richard Widmark had de slave Pops, not Johnny Wayne.

Gravel   It don't matter. Cha, Gravel finish wid yu.

Dennis   Gravel finish wid yu, Gravel tell yu why, Gravel go mek us all rich. Why should Dennis listen to yu?

Gravel   Yu wan' go, go.

Dennis   I will.

Gravel   Gravel say no more to yu. (*Goes inside.*)

Dennis   Good. I going to England! (**Hope** *comes outside.*) Hey Mama, Mama? Who star wid Errol Flynn in *Robin Hood* in 1939 . . . ?

Hope *slaps his face.*

Dennis   Sorry.

Hope   Wat yu sorry fer?

Dennis   Fer wat I done. Yu wan' tell me wat it is?

Hope   Yu see Pammy lately?

Dennis   Mama don't start.

Hope   Dat mean no.

Dennis   I juss had Pops man, I'll tell her.

Hope   Yu know wat she telling people? She pregnant, yu is de fudda!

Dennis   Wat?

Hope   Bwoy have I not tell a thousand times, to use summin?

Dennis   I didn't think.

Hope   I know yu didn't think!

Dennis   It all happen quick, I didn't have time . . .

Hope   Don' tell me I don' wan' to know.

Dennis   I gotta see her man.

Hope   Yu mad? She blaming yu, when it could be a whole line a men.

Dennis   Pammy not like dat.

Hope   Oh come on.

Dennis   She's not.

Hope   So wat yu sayin'?

Dennis   De baby mine. I know it.

Hope   It money she after.

Dennis   Oh Mama!

Hope   Fine don' listen to me, throw away yer life.

Dennis   I tell yu Pammy not like . . .

Hope   . . . like that! An' I tellin' yu from de moment me lay eyes pon de gyal I see trouble. Yu got all yer money saved Dennis, wat yu tink go happen if de child is yours? Leave it, let sum oder fool tek care a her, yu got dreams, plans, yu wan' throw it all away?

Dennis   No but. . . .

Hope   Deh is no but Dennis. I nuh raise yu to be like everyone else right. Ca' I tellin' yu years from now, when I sittin' in de theatre and I see yer name, yer face up on de big screen, I wan' to jump up and shout at all dem fools, and say das my bwoy! Im done it! Im special. Yu special Dennis?

Dennis   Yeah bu . . .

Hope   Dennis! Yu special?

Dennis   Yes Mama.

Hope   Right. Not a word to yer fudda.

Scene Three

Back yard. Night time. **Pammy** *is alone, drunk, and screaming her head off.*

Pammy   Dennis! I wan' to talk to yu. Don't ignore me bwoy! Dennis! Dennis! Denni . . .

Hope *comes out of the house.*

Pammy   I wan' to see Dennis.

Hope   Hush up Pamela, yu know wat time it is? Im not here.

Pammy   Dennis!

Hope   Gyal yu drunk?

Pammy   Wat yu care?

Hope   Yu supposed to be pregnant, yu don't know drink could harm de baby?

Pammy   Dennis . . .

Hope   Sweetheart I know wat yu goin' through.

Pammy   Move! 'Bout yu pretendin' yu nice. Yu couldn't wait to tell im.

Hope   Why didn't yu?

Pammy   Dis is between me an' Dennis.

Hope   Yu really tink my son go marry yu, whore like yer moder.

Pammy *makes a run at her.* **Hope** *holds her down.*

Hope   Yu wan' fight me Pamela? How much money yu wan'? How much yu wan' to get rid a it? Wat yu tink go happen here? Dennis give up im whole life juss to be wid yu? Men like Dennis are birds Pammy, deh have to spread dem wings and fly, not get lock up in a cage, wat we have to hold dem back. Wat we have to offer dem? Wat yu have dat de rest a us don' have Pammy? Yu got nuttin right. How much?

Gravel (*coming out*)   Hope! Stop it. Stop it! It awright Pammy, it awright. How long yu know?

Pammy   A few weeks.

Gravel   So why yu nuh say nuttin before?

Pammy   He'll tink I did it on purpose.

Gravel   It tek two to mek baby Pammy.

Pammy   Wally open im big mouth.

Gravel   Wally know as well? Look yu don' worry 'bout a ting right Pammy, we go wait right here fer Dennis and sort dis out.

Hope   No. Yu wan' ruin our son's life?

Gravel   I don' wan' hear anudda word from yu.

Hope   Yu talk to me like dat in front a her?

Gravel   Look at her Hope, look at her. Dis is yu yu nuh.

Hope   Don' tell her our business.

Gravel   Yu wan' her to go through wat yu did? Yu wan' her to sit at home wid baby, marry man she don't love perhaps, while she wait every night, pray fer Dennis to come tek her away? No Hope! Dis time no one get away.

Pammy   Hold on a second, yu not Dennis' fudda. (*Laughs.*)

Hope   I wan' break yer neck.

Pammy   Wa' wrong Hope, yu couldn' keep holda yer own man, he don' wan' yu? Serve yu right.

Gravel   Das enuff Pamela.

Pammy   Wat?

Gravel   Yu don' talk back to me wife like dat.

Pammy   Why yu so stupid? She mek fool a yu again yu, she doin' it now.

Hope   Throw de bitch out.

Pammy   Ask her 'bout her and Wally . . .

Hope   Throw her out Gravel.

Pammy   Ask her nuh man.

Gravel   Gravel know!

Pammy   An' yu nuh lick her in de head? I never wan' believe wat people say about yu.

Gravel   But yu did right? Come like de rest a dem, laugh at Gravel.

Pammy   I never laugh.

Gravel   Go home Pammy.

Pammy   Not once.

Gravel   Don' worry 'bout a ting right, Gravel sort dis out. Go home!

Gravel *hurries* **Pammy** *out.*

Hope   Yu don't know de baby his. Yu said yu let im go.

Gravel *switches on the car engine.*

Gravel   Hear dat? My son do dis. My son!

Hope   Yu really tink im go stay?

Gravel   Im have a heart Hope.

Hope   Are yu so stupid?

Gravel   Someware. Ware yu and Neville nuh have im. Im have a heart . . .

Hope *slaps his face.*

Gravel   See wat Neville do to yu.

Hope   Dis isn't about Neville. Jesus yu island men are all de same wid yer small minds and nuttin else, yu knew how me felt when we got married. Look 'pon yerself Gravel. Look 'pon yerself, yu really wan' Dennis to be like yu?

Gravel   Yu tink yer so special, but yer nuttin.

Hope   Bwoy like Neville, like im real fudda and yu can't stand dat!

Hope *turns round to see* **Dennis** *who arrived a moment earlier. He turns round and leaves the way he came.*

Hope   Dennis.

Scene Four

Back yard two days later. **Dennis** *enters, being pushed into the yard by* **Lester**.

Lester   I only bringing yer here ca' yer fudda is a friend, but if yu joke wid me again right, once more, I go bus' yer head an' throw yer arse in jail.

Dennis   So do it den. Tek me to jail. Yu fat rass . . .

Lester   Shut yer mout.

Dennis   It bottle a rum yu wan'. Yu juss like dem, liar.

Lester *(swings his baton)*   I'll do it yer nuh.

Gravel *comes out of the house.*

Lester   Gravel! Yu never guess ware me find im. On top a Wally Mitchell, deh were both beatin' each oder nearly half to death, Lord knows why. Deh mek aright mess a Joey's bar. I had to arrest im.

Gravel   Tek im den. (**Lester** *laughs.*) Yu hear me tell joke?

Lester   No. But I tought . . .

Gravel   Wat?

Lester *eyes* **Dennis** *laughing to himself.*

Lester   I hear yu get de car running? Lot a people tought yu couldn't do it. But not me. Gravel Gilbey got im fudda's hands. Dat was a nice bottle a rum yer give my fudda Gravel. Im bin talkin' 'bout it fer days.

Gravel   Deh's none left.

Lester   Well das a shame. I go have to tek im in Gravel.

Gravel   So tek im.

Lester   Awright. (*To* **Dennis**.) Come.

Gravel   I'll come wid yu.

Lester (*suspicious*)   Good.

Gravel   I tell yer captain how much yu an' yer fudda enjoyed my rum!

Lester   Juss yu keep an eye on im right. Ca' next time I bus' im head!

Gravel   So long Lester.

Lester *exits*.

Dennis   Yu wan' fer me to say tanks?

Gravel   Yer tink I wan' anyting from yu?

Dennis   Fine den.

Gravel   Good!

Dennis   Right!

Gravel *gets in the car*.

I hope yer crash.

Gravel   Wat?

Dennis   Nuttin.

Gravel   Yu 'fraid to speak up?

Dennis (*throws something*)   Present fer yu. Wally's front teet'. Ca' yu not man enough to do it yerself. Yu not even sorry.

Gravel   Sorry fer wat? Wat Gravel got to be sorry fer?

Dennis   If yu weren't sick man.

Gravel   Yer punch me out? Gravel de one who should be doing de punching round here. Yu see Pammy?

Dennis   Don' change de subject.

Gravel   Have yu?

Dennis   No.

Gravel   I see.

Dennis   Yeah Pops yu see, I Neville Gilbey's bwoy right, das wat yu see. Me juss like im. Yu call yerself a man?

Gravel   Man? Yu is a man Dennis?

Dennis   More than yu!

Gravel   Yes so all dis time I see yu, actin' all nice and sweet wid dat gyal, waitin' to get wat yu wan'. An' when yu finally get it, when she need yu de most, yu throw her away like sum rubbish, oh yes Dennis, yu are a man.

Dennis   It weren't like dat.

Gravel   Yu don' love de gyal.

Dennis   I do.

Gravel   So badly yu wan' leave her?

Dennis   Wat am I supposed to do den, yu tell me.

Gravel   Yu do wass right.

Dennis   Pops I can't.

Gravel   Den yu is nuttin.

Dennis   Stop lookin' at me like I im right. I don't even know de man.

Gravel   Yu his son.

Dennis   Yu my fudda. Wat I am is ca' a yu.

Gravel   Wat yu are is ca' a im, ca' a yer mudda . . .

Dennis   And yu!

Gravel *starts the car up.*

Dennis   Yeah gw'n den!

A loud bang from the engine. Smoke rises from the bonnet. **Dennis** *shouts his father's name as he runs over to him. He pulls him out of the car.*

Gravel   Yu tell me yu fix it! (**Dennis** *laughs.*) Shut up.

Dennis   I mus be yer son Pops.

Gravel   Useless!

Dennis   Like yu.

Gravel (*shakes his head*)   Neville's bwoy.

Dennis   I yer bwoy.

Gravel   Neville's bwoy!

Dennis   I wan' act Pops, I wan' life! Ain't dat why yu went England, to get life? I awready tell people I going man. If I stay, deh go laugh at me too, hear dem now, Gravel wife and im nephew Wally . . .

Gravel   Shut yer mout!

Dennis   I don' wan' dat.

Gravel   It wat yu feel inside dat matters.

Dennis   Why yu have to come back? Yu can't you see wat it done to yu? Well I not go die here like yu. Mama could be right yer nuh, how yu know it my baby? Pammy a Simpson, she juss like she mudda.

Gravel   Yu really believe dat?

Dennis   Yes!

Gravel   Den on yer way Neville's bwoy. Gravel try and give yu an' yer mudda a decent life and look wat yer do wid it. Gravel come back ca' a de two a yu. Yu know how long I was in Englan' before Neville decide to tell me she was pregnant? A year! An' like a fool me come back, ca' like a fool me marry her, ca' like a stupid fool Gravel love her all im life. (*Takes a deep breath.*)

Dennis   Pops?

Gravel   Dennis gw'n inside and get me my medicine.

Dennis   Wat?

Gravel   I'll fetch it myself. (*Clutches his heart.*)

Dennis   Pops!

Dennis *runs inside the house. He comes back out with* **Gravel**'*s tablets.*

Dennis   Come on Pops, yer not sick, yu juss worked up a lickle right? Pops? I go fetch de doctor. (**Gravel** *holds his son's hand.*) Lemme go Pops, lemme go man.

Dennis *runs out.*

Gravel (*in pain*)   God! (*Feels the last beat in his heart.*) Hope?

Scene Five

Back yard. One week later. **Little Hope** *is alone on stage polishing the car.* **Dennis** *comes out to help her.* **Little Hope** *grabs his rag and throws it to the ground.* **Dennis** *picks it up,* **Little Hope** *grabs it from him again and does the same thing.*

Dennis   I only tryin' to help Lickle Hope.

Little Hope (*snaps*)   Hope! Stop calling me Lickle Hope.

Dennis   Sorry. (*Picks up his rag.*)

Little Hope   I cleaning Daddy's car! Leave it. Yu aways mek im upset. Yu kill im. I hate yu.

Dennis   Yu go get yer dress all dirty.

Little Hope   Daddy aways let me wear pants.

Little Hope *walks to the house, she passes* **Pammy** *who gently taps her on the head.*

Little Hope   I look like doll to yu?

Pammy   No.

Little Hope   Yu stupid?

Dennis   Hey, Lickle Hope.

Little Hope   My name is Hope!

Dennis (*snaps*)   Get inside.

Pammy *watches* **Dennis** *polishing the car.*

Dennis   Tought I might tek it out yu nuh, see how it go.

Pammy   Good.

Dennis   Wan' come?

Pammy   Awright.

Dennis   Little Hope said I kill im, she right yer nuh?

Pammy   Don't say dat.

Dennis   I keep seein' im face Pammy.

Pammy   Don't.

Dennis   Pay no attention right, Dennis juss upset.

Dennis *sees* **Hope** *standing by the door, watching. This prompts him to kiss* **Pammy** *on the lips.*

Pammy   Dennis . . .

Dennis *kisses her again.*

Leave de car fer a minute.

Hope   Yu wan' summin from de store Dennis?

Dennis   Car look good yu tink?

Pammy   Yes.

Hope   Do yu wan' summin from de store Dennis?

Dennis   Watch me now Pops.

Hope   Sooner or later yu go have to speak to me.

Pammy   Come Dennis let's go fer a ride now.

Hope   Look at me.

Pammy   Juss leave im.

Hope   Dennis?

Dennis   I not sellin' de car Mama.

Hope   Yu hear me say yu should?

Dennis   Yu can't wait to get rid a everyting that was Pops can yu?

Hope   I loved yer fudda.

Dennis   Hear dat Pammy, she loved Pops.

Hope   I haven't got de strength to fight yu awright.

Dennis   Juss get me a bokkle a pop from de shop and leave me alone right.

Hope   I soon come.

Dennis   So wat about me bin so special den? Dat lie too?

Hope   Wat yu wan' fer me to say?

Dennis   I not Neville's bwoy, I can't be, I Gravel's bwoy right?

Hope   Yer no one's bwoy Dennis, yu belong to yerself.

Dennis   Whose am I Mama? Juss tell me dat, or yu don't know.

Hope *walks out of the yard without saying anything.*

Pammy   I hate her. I know she yer mama but I really hate her . . .

Dennis   Awright Pammy, wa wrong wid yu? Yu have me.

Pammy   Have I?

Dennis (*snaps*)   Yes!

Pammy   How yu feel Dennis?

Dennis   Fine, juss fine. Wat, yu don' believe me?

Pammy   I wan' to.

Dennis   'But soft, what light through yonder window breaks? It is the East, and Juliet is the sun!'

Pammy   Come inside. Dennis?

Dennis *finds a piece of wood and paints something on it.*

Pammy   Dennis? Dennis!

Dennis *can hear but ignores her.* **Pammy** *leaves the yard. Dennis finishes painting. The sign now reads,* Gravel & Sons. **Dennis** *places it against the car window. He stares at it.*

End.

The No Boys Cricket Club

The No Boys Cricket Club was first performed at the Theatre Royal, Stratford East, London, on 24 May 1996. The cast was as follows:

Abi	Donna Croll
Masie	Anni Domingo
Danni	Michele Joseph
Michael	Steve Toussaint
Faye	Nina Conti
Young Abi	Ashley Miller
Young Masie	Sharon Duncan Brewster
Ferdy Watson	Jason Rose
Jenny	Natasha Gordon
Shirley	Karlene Saunders
Cita	Trixie Munyama

Reece, Miss Devereaux and the Clanton Street Boys were played by members of the cast.

Directed by Indhu Rubasingham
Designed by Rosa Maggiora
Lighting by Chris Davey

Characters

Abi, 53
Danni, 19, Abi's daughter
Michael, 26, Abi's son
Faye, 21
Masie, 53
Ferdy, Masie's husband
Young Abi
Young Masie
Jenny
Shirley ⎬ The No Boys Cricket Club
Cita
Reece, Faye's boyfriend
Miss Devereaux
The Clanton Street Boys

The play is set in the garden of a council house in present-day London and in Kingston Town, Jamaica, 1958.

Act One

Scene One

Abi *enters from the house, carrying a bag of washing. She hangs the clothes on the washing line, she looks up when she hears voices somewhere. Voices of young girls playing cricket. She looks around and can see something.*

Abi   Jenny Vincent, no, man, no.

Shirley (*offstage*)   You're out, out . . .

Jenny (*offstage*)   Oh shut up, ya breath come like frog . . .

Shirley (*offstage*)   Out, out out!

Abi   Oh yeah, go on girl, go on.

Sound of a cricket ball being hit. **Abi** *laughs out.*

Cita (*offstage*)   Run na girl . . .

All the girls cheer. They call out the name **Abi**.

Abi (*to audience*)   That game had me buzzing like some bee for the whole week. It was sunny, we reserved the field two weeks in advance and I was on serious form. Me, Abigail Rosemary Sandford.

Sound of another ball being whacked.

Straight up, you see it, boom! We were playing class 2C, throughout the week during schoolbreaks, and we were beating the pants off them. They could only get twelve runs out of us when they were up. Today was our last day, and soon we go put them out of misery forever, soon.

A school bell is rung. The girls cheer.

Young Masie (*offstage*)   Abi girl you were on fire!

Young Abi (*offstage*)   Y' think so Masie?

Young Masie (*offstage*)   Oh stop it, you know so. You country girls are summin else. I'm still waiting for that last ball to come down.

Young Abi (*offstage*)   Must be in Frankfield by now.

Young Masie (*offstage*)   Na, Guyana.

Young Abi (*offstage*)   Florida!

Miss Devereaux (*offstage*)   Masie Williams, Abigail Sandford, would you girls mind gracing me with your presence in the classroom?

Young Abi/Young Masie (*offstage*)   Coming Miss Devereaux.

Abi (*laughs. Then stares at something.*)   Yes?

The voices fade away as loud popular music comes blaring out of the house. **Abi** *is slightly bewildered, but comes to.*

(*Yelling.*) Michael, will you turn the music down na man, Michael!

The music is turned down a bit. **Abi** *returns to her washing, but her peace is shortlived as she now hears yelling from the next door garden.*

Faye (*offstage*)   You lying bastard, you ain't going anywhere.

Reece (*offstage*)   I've had enough of your shit!

Abi (*to herself*)   Now they're gonna start up.

Faye (*offstage*)   You ain't going.

Abi   Shut up over there. (*To herself.*) Every blasted day!

Michael *pops his head out from one of the bedroom windows.*

Michael (*offstage*)   Mum, wat you yelling for, I've turned it down, ain't I?

Abi   Not you, them.

Michael (*offstage*)   They're at it again?

Abi   Where's Dannielle?

Michael (*offstage*)   In the bloody bathroom still, tell her to come out now Mum.

Abi   Do not swear Michael.

Michael   Just tell her, I gotta go out soon.

Abi   Keep her inside for me, I don't want her seeing this.

Michael   What they're yelling about now?

Abi   Michael if you want to talk to me, come out here please.

Michael   You come in here.

Abi   You wan' to eat in this house?

The neighbours are still at it.

Shut up!

Reece (*offstage*)   You dumb bitch, now you're bothering the neighbours.

Faye (*offstage*)   I don't care about her.

Abi   What she say?

Reece (*offstage*)   Gimme back my keys Faye.

Faye (*offstage*)   So go get them.

The door opens, a set of keys are tossed out.

Abi   But Jesus Christ.

Reece (*offstage*)   You're gonna go right out and get them back.

Faye (*offstage*)   You're the one who wants to go out with that slag.

Reece (*offstage*)   There's only one slag I know, an' I'm looking at her.

Abi   Damn right.

Faye (*offstage*)   You bastard . . .

Michael (*offstage*)   Go get my keys!

Faye (*offstage*)   Go screw!

Sound of the girl being slapped. **Faye** *comes out, picks up the keys, and walks back in, coldly acknowledging* **Abi**.

Faye   Yes?

Faye *goes back in.*

Abi   About she don't care what I think, we'll soon see when the council drag her arse out, she'll care plenty then, plenty.

Michael *comes out bare-chested.*

Michael   Mum, who are you talking to?

Abi (*slightly embarrassed*)   Don't stand out like that in the cold Michael, you catch cold. What do you want?

Michael (*delves into the basket, takes out some socks*)   That and that.

Abi   They're not dry yet.

Michael   They'll be alright, once over with an iron.

Abi   You mean to say you've got no clean socks in your room?

Michael   No.

Abi   Boy have no shame. Where you going in such a hurry?

Michael   Out.

Abi   Out where?

Michael   Out there, I don't ask you about your business Mum.

Abi   What business is that, apart from cleaning up after you pikne?

Michael   'Lord nobody don't love me!'

Abi   Only people that give me the time of day is gas, electric an' telephone. You see the bill?

Michael   You'll get my share, but there is Danni as well you know.

Abi   She's studying.

Michael   She's a pain. She ain't getting her room back.

Abi   Oh not this again.

Michael   It was mine to begin with, she shouldn't have leaped in there in the first place.

Abi   Alright, alright, but I still want money from you.

Michael   Yeah soon Mum, I'm skint right now.

Abi   Skint? Of course you're skint, with your 80-pound trainers.

Michael   They don't cost 80 quid Mum.

Abi   Don't take me for a fool. I see your friend Gary Warren wid the same pair, he told me how much they cost, 80 pounds. (*Raises her foot.*) You see these, £2.99 from the market, 1984. Spend any of your money on Patrick?

Michael   I was wondering when you were gonna start with that.

Abi   Well have you?

Michael   Leave it Mum.

Abi   Should be ashamed.

Michael   Patrick will get money when I'm good and ready, you'll get money when I'm good and ready. (*Under his breath.*) For fuck's sake . . . (*Goes inside.*)

Abi   Don't swear at me Michael. If your father was alive today he'd . . .

Michael (*cutting off*) . . . give me two good licks in my head!

Michael *comes back out with some letters.*

Michael　There's a letter for you. (*Hands it over.*) I've got two.

Abi　That's nice.

Michael　Do you want the stamps?

Abi　If you like.

Michael　Christ. Here. (*Gives them to her.*)

Abi　Thank you kind sir.

Michael　It's alright.

Abi (*reads the back of her letter*)　But Jesus Christ! Masie Williams, so it's now you decide to write to me girl!

Abi *tears open the letter.*

Michael　Who's Masie?

Abi　Your Aunt Masie.

Michael　Yeah, you want to narrow that down for me?

Abi　Your Aunt Masie from Streatham.

Michael　We ain't got family in Streatham.

Abi　Yes you do.

Michael　Who?

Abi (*irritated*)　Your Aunt Masie.

Michael　Oh man!

Abi　You remember your Uncle Ferdy, her husband, and Claudia, Jeffrey and Vanessa.

Michael　More cousins. Nice. They from Dad's side?

Abi　No!

Michael　Then how is she my aunt?

Abi　We grew up back home.

Michael Oh home, yeah and so?

Abi So she is like a sister, she's your elder, you treat her with respect.

Michael I ain't even met her.

Abi Oh go about your business and let me read my letter.

A loud banging on a door is heard from inside.

Danni (*offstage*) Mum!

Abi Lord Jesus, once, just once, can I have some peace in my own home?

Michael Must be Danni, Mum.

Abi Dannielle stop your noise. What is wrong with that girl?

Michael Me locking her in the bathroom might have summin to do with it.

Abi Why did you do that?

Michael You told me to!

Abi Boy how old are you, don't answer that. Go and open the door.

Michael *curses as he goes back in.* **Abi** *tries to get back to her letter but is disturbed yet again when* **Faye** *comes out carrying a stack of records; she tosses them on to the floor.* **Abi** *looks up, they glare at each other.*

Faye Yes!

Abi *kisses her teeth.*

Danni (*offstage*) Wass the bloody matter with you?

Michael (*offstage*) Mum told me to do it.

Danni (*offstage*) Where is she?

Abi *stops reading. She folds the letter and waits for her daughter* **Danni** *who enters wearing a bathrobe.*

Danni   Mum what you playing at, why you telling him to lock me in the bathroom?

Abi   I didn't . . .

At this point, **Faye** *comes out again, carrying more records. She dumps them with the others.*

Danni   Faye, Faye?

Abi   Don't go over there. Dannielle Carter.

Danni *climbs over.*

Abi   I see, this is what you do when I tell you not to do things.

Danni   He hit her again, why didn't you say?

Abi   But what's it got to do with you?

Faye *comes out,* **Danni** *blocks her path.*

Danni   Faye what's this all about?

Faye   I don't want a single thing in here belonging to that bastard, I don't want nothing.

Danni   What's he done? Faye!

Faye   Jackie Willis come tell me, to my face right, that she saw Reece and some young slag at a rave together, an' they weren't just chatting.

Danni   You know what Jackie's like.

Faye   I know what Reece is like as well.

Danni   You don't know that.

Faye   You an expert on men or summin?

Abi   Hey, young lady, she is the only friend you have.

Danni   Mum for chrissake.

Abi (*to* **Danni**)   When are you going to wake up to her child? Look I got a letter from your Aunt Masie.

Danni   Triffic. Why don't you sit down with it and be quiet Mum.

Abi   Don't talk to me like I'm some fool girl.

Faye   Last time he does that to me.

Danni   You've said that before.

Faye   I've never thrown out his records before.

Danni   He'll slap you around again.

Faye   You reckon? (*Goes back in.*)

Danni   Faye?

Faye *comes back carrying a knife.*

Danni   Fuck.

Faye   Thass right, he ain't gonna hit me no more.

Danni   As soon as you've sobered up, he'll grab it off ya.

Faye   Well what else can I do, Miss Know-all?

Danni   Leave him.

Faye   And go where?

Abi   She's not coming here.

Faye   Did I ask?

Danni   Mum stay out of it.

Abi   Your Aunt Masie has a daughter, Claudia, 19 years old, four 'A' levels, (*in* **Faye**'s *direction*) 'A' levels!

Faye   Whoopee fuckin' do!

Abi   Dannielle, what did she just say to me?

Danni   Nothing.

Abi   She's a smart young lady, got a baby girl.

Faye   Can't be that smart then.

Danni   Mum is there any point to this?

Abi   I'm just telling you about your Aunt Masie's children.

Danni   I ain't got a Aunt Masie.

Faye *grunts in laughter.*

Faye   Your Mum's gone, big time.

Danni   Rub it in, why don't ya. Come on Faye.

Faye *hands over the knife.* **Abi** *is no longer listening to them. She is shaken by something she has read.*

Faye   I fuckin' hate him Danni, I deserve better than this.

Danni   I know.

Faye   Mum won't even come round to see us because of him. Now she wants me to move back in with them, no bloody way!

Danni   She's alright half the time.

Faye   You an expert on mothers now?

Danni   No.

Faye   I don't know how you can stand living with yours. Look at her, look. You want to grow up to be like that?

Danni   Not so loud.

Danni *watches her mother.*

Faye   No wonder Shanelle is running you down.

Danni   Alright Faye!

Faye   You know what she's saying, about your family, Michael. That you're all dealing in it. (*Laughs.*) Ain't true is it?

Danni   No it bloody ain't!

Faye's *front door is slammed.*

Faye   That's him out for the night. (*Sound of a baby crying.*)
Now he has to fuckin' start. (*Shouting.*) I'm coming alright! So
what are you going to do about Shanelle?

Danni   I'll see to it.

Faye   Nice one, give her a kick in the head for me.

Faye *goes back in,* **Danni** *climbs back over.*

Danni   You made me look bad Mum, don't you ever stop,
Mum?

Abi   I'm sorry what did you say?

Danni   Nuttin forget it.

Danni *goes back in, but not before* **Michael** *passes her and taps
her on the head.*

Danni   Move!

Michael   Or what! Mum, do this tie for me, one of your
special knots nice and loose yeah Mum, come on, quick
time.

Abi   Yes, yes, alright.

Michael   You alright? Mum are you alri . . .

Abi   Yes I'm fine. So where are you off to?

Michael   Just out. No, that's too tight, do it again.

Abi   Out with your friends, wasting time on foolishness,
should be ashamed.

Michael   Now that's too loose, come on Mum.

Abi   I'm trying.

Michael   Try harder.

Abi   What kind of tie is this? (*Reading.*) Guchy, gucky,
what?

Michael   Gucci.

Abi   Wasting your money, ain't seen my grandson in months.

Michael   Will you come off that please?

Abi   A Gucci tie instead of Patrick, you want to get your priorities straight.

Michael   The bloody tie Mum.

Abi *tightens it, almost choking* **Michael**.

Abi   You should treasure every moment to be with him, how long do you think that lasts, how long?

Michael (*pushing her away*)   Forget the tie, I'll do it myself. Wass the matter wid you?

Abi   Your Aunt Masie. Her boy Jeffrey, he's gone.

Michael   Gone where?

Abi   He's dead, Jeffrey's dead.

Abi *begins to sob.*

Michael   Oh man, oh chriss Mum, juss hang on. (*Calling.*) Oi ugly, ugly!

Danni   I got a name shithead.

Michael   Never mind your name, go make some tea quick time.

Danni   You got hands.

Michael   It's for Mum.

Abi   No I don't . . .

Danni   She's got hands.

Michael   Put the kettle on now!

Danni   Go get one of your girlfriends pregnant!

Michael   You fuckin' little . . .

Abi   Michael stop your swearing.

Michael   Tea on its way Mum, right Danni!

Abi   I don't want any blasted tea.

Michael   Yeah but I just . . . alright.

Abi   I have to go, right now . . . Masie needs me, I have to go.

Michael   Yeah, course.

Danni   Tea will soon be ready Mum, oh yeah ignore me why don't you.

Danni *enters, she sees her brother.*

Danni   What's up with Mum?

Michael   Bad news from Aunt Masie.

Danni (*irritated*)   Who's Aunt Masie?

Michael   Fucked if I know.

Scene Two

The cricket pitch, Kingston. **Abi** *is watching* **Young Masie** *getting ready to bowl.*

Abi   Masie Williams was the captain of our little team and my best friend ever. She never had much. Mother ran off when she was just a baby. So she went from one relative to the other. Everyone thought she'd turn out bad, but she was the fastest bowler I ever saw. Lord could she bowl, Jesus!

As soon as **Young Masie** *bowls, lights fully on cricket field.* **Young Masie** *has just bowled out* **Young Abi**.

Young Masie   You're out, out, out!

Young Abi   Yes alright Masie.

Young Masie   Got to take the highs with the lows Abi.

Young Abi   I know, I'm just glad you're bowling for us.

Young Masie   I'm glad you're glad. But we couldn't do it without you you know.

Young Abi   We are just a little team Masie, summin for fun, after school.

Young Masie   Summin for fun! Listen girl you know what Dedee Jones' brother Smokey have the nerve to say to me the other day?

Young Abi   No but you're going to tell me.

Young Masie   He says him and his boys from Clanton Street can beat us in a game, us! (*Laughs.*)

Young Abi   You didn't challenge him did you?

Young Masie   A few weeks from now.

Young Abi   Oh Masie girl!

Young Masie   Come on we can beat them.

Young Abi   We got exams coming, you said we wouldn't play till the vacations.

Young Masie   We'll start practising this weekend.

Young Abi   No, we can't.

Young Masie   Why not?

Young Abi   Weekends is when Daddy comes back from the country.

Young Masie   And when was the last time you seen him?

Young Abi   He said he would this time. He's bringing me back a present.

Young Masie   He won't.

Young Abi   He will!

Young Masie   We need you.

Young Abi   He needs me. Oh you make it so difficult sometimes. He's my only real family Masie. I shouldn't be wasting time with this foolishness.

Young Masie   That's Miss Tyler talking.

Young Abi   Don't say that woman's name to me.

Young Masie   Miss Tyler, Miss Tyler . . .

Young Abi   Stop it!

Young Masie   I'm right though. Ain't right, things she says to you, ain't right at all.

Young Abi   She was Moma's sister.

Young Masie   Don't excuse her.

Young Abi   She blames me.

Young Masie   Tell her to go to hell.

Young Abi   What!

Young Masie   Yes!! You're Abigail Sandford, and you should do what you want to do, am I right?

Young Abi   Like, play for the team?

Young Masie   Why not?

Young Abi   Yeah you're Abigail Sandford, and you should do what you want, just as long as it's what Masie Williams wants.

Young Masie   Hold on a minute. You're our star player girl, it's truth. You say your daddy loves cricket? Well bring him along, let him watch, but he can't coach us.

Young Abi (*pleading*)   Masie . . .

Young Masie (*pleading*)   Abi . . .

Young Abi   Look, we'll see, but I'm not promising anything.

Young Masie   Thank you darling, you'll never let me down.

Young Abi   Hold on I didn't say for definite . . . (**Young Masie** *starts packing up.*) Wat is it with you girl, you want to rule the world or something?

Young Masie   Good idea.

Young Abi   What's the hurry?

Young Masie   Ferdy Watson was pulling my hair in class today.

Young Abi   And Miss Devereaux put him in a corner, and you kicked him in the arse all the way home, so?

Young Masie   We ran past Miss Stuart, nearly knocked her out of her stool, you know wat they say about her, how she's never wrong about anything. She told me one day me and Ferdy Watson are going get married, have children, can you think of anything more disgusting, Ferdy's kids? Well she is wrong about this, it won't happen girl, you hear me? But you carry on, you wanna end up with Teddy Carter, thass your business.

Young Abi   Teddy Carter g'way!

Young Masie   I saw that sweet he passed you, you country girls think you're so sly.

Young Abi   He wants to join the team.

Young Masie   I hope you said no.

Young Abi   He's good with a bat.

Young Masie   We are not called the No Boys Cricket Club for nothing Abi.

Young Abi   Look I've seen the way those Clanton boys play.

Young Masie   We can beat them.

Young Abi   Why is this so important?

Young Masie   If you coulda seen the way old man Rivers was laughing when he heard about the game, he says if we win, he'll put our picture on the front of the paper.

Young Abi   Front?

Young Masie   Front page!

Young Abi   Don't wish for the impossible Masie.

Young Masie   There's nothing wrong with wishing. We're going places Abi I can feel it and no stupid gang of boys is going to mess this up you hear me?

Scene Three

London, five days later. **Michael** *comes from the alleyway and places bags of drugs under the plantpots.* **Danni** *comes out.*

Danni   What are you up to?

Michael   Get lost.

Danni   You bloody liar.

Michael   Say that again? Y' think I don't know your game, you're lucky I don't bust your head now. I suppose I have to hide these in my room now, you so fuckin' nosey. (*He stashes them in his pocket.*) How do I look?

Danni   Like someone with bags of drugs stuffed in their pocket.

Michael   You're not funny.

Danni   Just walk through quickly.

Michael   She'll spot these a mile off.

Danni   Doubt it. Mum and Aunt Masie are now talking about where to get the best Jamaican patties from – London or Birmingham.

Michael   Na, she can't help herself but ask. I ain't got time for a scene with her.

Danni   Scared.

Michael   Not as scared as you will be.

Danni   I ain't afraid of you Michael.

Michael   No? (*Prodding her.*)

Danni   No!

Michael   How did Mum and Dad ever have such a weakling of a kid.

Danni   Oh don't put yourself down broth.

Michael   There goes your mouth again, you ever wonder why you get into so much trouble?

Danni   I know why.

Michael   Oh let me guess, because of your big bad brother?

Danni   Why can't you piss off? Everyone knows about you Michael. You ain't that clever the only one who don't know nuttin is Mum.

Michael   Well let's do our best to keep it from her. I'm out of here.

Danni   Don't get picked up by the police now?

Michael (*laughs*)   You and your mouth.

Michael *leaves through the alleyway.* **Danni** *sits on the steps leading up to the house. She reads her paper.* **Abi**, *and* **Masie**, *come out. They nearly trip over* **Danni**.

Abi   Oh will you stop with that . . .

Masie   I'm telling you girl . . .

Abi   Dannielle, don't sit there, you tryin' to kill us?

Masie   Those fools they got playing for us don't know nuttin about cricket, letting those stupid white boys beat them. Especially that big ugly one that's always in the papers, with the moustache, whatshisname? You think he coulda bowled out Abigail Sandford, no way! This was you. (*Pretending to bat.*) Pow, and pow another pow!

Abi   Masie shush.

Masie   No, and you went pow!

Abi   Alright.

Danni   Whass all this?

Masie   Whass all this? Child you mean to say you didn't know your mother was a devil wid a bat?

Danni   No.

Masie   She was the best, she go like this, pow and pow!

Abi   Stop your noise.

Masie (*laughs*)   You know it's true.

Abi   Yes!

Danni   You used to play cricket Mum?

Masie   We didn't just play Dannielle, we lived. Wan' to hear about it?

Abi   Not right now Masie.

Masie (*pleading*)   Abi . . .

Abi   No! Where are you going?

Danni   What makes you think I'm going anywhere?

Abi   Your face. I want to talk to you.

Danni   Will it take long?

Abi   As long as it needs to. I saw your friend Shanelle today.

Danni   Did you?

Abi   She says she's looking forward to seeing you.

Danni   Good.

Abi   I don't like that girl, she's got too much to say for herself.

Danni   Great, you don't like Shanelle you don't like Faye.

Abi   What's going on Dannielle?

Masie   Let her go Abi.

Danni   Thank you Aunt Masie.

Abi   Just tell me.

Danni   Mum I'm seeing a friend from college, you'll like her, five 'A' levels and goes to church every Sunday, can I go?

Abi   You think I'm stupid?

Danni   Why would I think that Mum?

Abi   If it was raining right now but Faye said it was sunny, would you run out arse-naked?

Danni   Can I go?

Abi   I'm trying to help you.

Danni   Yeah right.

Abi   Don't!

Masie   Come on Abi.

Abi   Masie please.

Masie   You remember that time when we went out fishing wid the Brewster boys? All the girls warned us not to go, but we went anyway.

Danni   Later Mum.

Abi   Danni . . .

Masie We shoulda worn iron bras.

Danni Mum I'm just . . . (*Realising what* **Masie** *has said.*) You wat!

Abi Nothing! (*Ushering her out.*) Just go about your business, Danni. And don't slam the . . . (*Door is slammed.*) door.

Masie (*feeling* **Abi***'s glare*)   Did I do something wrong?

Abi There was no need for her to hear a story like that.

Masie Oh come on, don't you hear wat they say nowadays? Seen it, heard it, bought the t-shirt. They're gonna do what they want so let them get on with it.

Abi You don't mean that.

Masie Oh yes I do. When Claudia was thirteen, I caught her leaving the house with some big red lipstick on her face, my lipstick, I told her 'Girl you best wipe that off'. Hear wat she says, 'Oh but Mum, Tina's mum lets her wear make-up'. (**Abi** *laughs*.) It's true . . .

Abi . . . 'It isant fair . . .'

Masie 'Tina's mum lets her do whatever she wants . . .'

Abi Not just mums though. What about the fathers? Michael would always make me look bad in front of his daddy.

Masie That's Jeffrey and Ferdy all over, the tings that boy would get himself into, just to prove to his daddy how big and tough he is. They do it anyway, so why bother yourself. Abi? You're staring at me girl what is it?

Abi It's strange to hear you talk, like he was still alive.

Masie I know my boy is dead Abi.

Abi I'm sorry.

Masie It's alright.

Abi Oh Masie, what can I say to make it better huh? (*She takes her hand.*) It's good to see you.

Masie It's good to be seen. Thanks for coming to the funeral.

Abi Oh hush.

Masie You know, even at the reception, his mother still found time to turn up her nose at the food.

Abi She lost her only grandson.

Masie No, it goes deeper than that. You know, on my wedding day, I found her in my room, packing my clothes, she had my cricket bat thrown in the dustbin, dustbin!

Abi You want some more juice? (**Abi** *goes into the kitchen.*)

Masie 'No more time for foolishness girl, you marrying my boy, that carry responsibilities.' Only thing she ever bin right about. We didn't wish hard enough girl.

Abi We were young we thought we could rule the world, or you did.

Masie Don't you think we could of? What happened to our plans Abi, the club?

Abi How's Ferdy?

Masie Ferdy?

Abi Your husband.

Masie You're still hiding girl, at your age.

Abi I'm just asking how he is.

Masie Ferdy's fine.

Abi He can't be just *fine*! I mean you sure he doesn't mind you staying here for a while? You should be together now.

Masie Save your sympathy Abigail, Ferdy won't be lonely.

Sound of people calling out the name Shanelle.

Masie   What's wrong.

Abi   Nothing.

Masie   Are you sure?

Abi   I'm fed up. Oh Masie, is this what it feels like?

Masie   What?

Abi   Getting old?

Masie   I don't know. Stand up.

Abi   Excuse me?

Masie   Stand up I say.

Abi   For what?

Masie   I'm tired of letting you make me feel miserable.

Abi   I'm doing that?

Masie   Yes, now stand up! Right, come on let's play.

Abi   We can't, not no more.

Masie   This will make everything better. You see that plank, that's our bat. (*Rolls up* **Danni**'s *paper.*) And this our ball.

Abi   I can't do this.

Masie   Stand over there, be ready to hit that ball, score a six like the old days.

Abi   Masie, I can't do it.

Masie   Eye on the ball, like Charlie Bennett say.

Abi   Are you listening to me?

Masie   No now bat.

Abi   Masie . . .

Masie   I'm bowling.

Masie *bowls,* **Abi** *misses completely.*

Abi   You see?

Masie   You know wat your problem is?

Abi   No but you're gonna tell me.

Masie   You stopped wishing. (*Looking around.*) In a big way. I bat. (*They exchange places.*)

Abi   You know how I feel.

Masie   I can't believe you are still twisting up inside over that. Miss Tyler has been dead for years, why are you still letting her get to you?

Abi   Don't say that woman's name to me!

Masie   Miss Tyler, oh Miss Tyler!

Abi   Stop it.

Masie (*indicating where she wants the ball to be thrown*)   Look just give it to me there, if you can manage that.

Abi   I suppose you never stopped wishing.

Masie   Never. Bowl.

Abi   No! I gotta get dinner ready.

Masie   Gotta go hide you mean.

Abi   If you like!

Abi *leaves.* **Masie** *smiles to herself. She's still got it. She waves the bat a bit more, hitting imaginary ball.*

Masie   Pow, pow, pow! The No Boys Cricket Club! (*Laughs.*)

Masie *stops playing when she sees a badly beaten up* **Danni** *followed by* **Faye**.

Masie   Oh lord what happened here?

Faye   Nuttin, she fell over.

Masie   Girl don't gimme that, I know a beat up girl when I see one.

Faye   What do you know?

Masie   What's your mama gonna say?

Faye   Don't tell her, I don't want her startin' on me.

Abi *comes out.*

Abi   Dannielle, oh my God Dannielle.

Danni   Now don't start Mum I can explain.

Abi   No need. Gangfights Masie, that's what it's about, damn stupid brawling for stupid girls.

Danni   Mum will you leave it.

Abi   No child I will not leave it. (*To* **Faye**.) This is all your fault.

Faye   Of course.

Abi   I don't see no blood on you.

Faye   I wasn't fighting.

Abi   Of course!

Faye   I'm outta here. (*Climbing over the fence.*)

Abi   Yes, don't you have a baby to look after?

Faye   See you tomorrow Danni. (*Enters her house.*)

Abi   Come here. (*Checking her face.*)

Danni   Mum don't fuss.

Abi   Keep still.

Danni (*pushing her away*)   I'm OK! You always showing me up?

Abi   Me?

Danni   You!

Abi   Well you're the one who's been fighting.

Danni   Why do you keep making a show of me, why do you let Michael run rings around you?

Abi   I'm your mother, you answer my questions.

Danni   Shanelle was slagging you off, and it's not just her.

Abi   That's no excuse for brawling on the streets like some dirty animal.

Danni   Oh Mum will you stop, come on you must know what I'm talking about. You can't be that stupid.

Abi   Don't you . . .

Danni   Well are you?

Abi   I don't want you seeing that Faye anymore.

Danni   Yeah that's it, turn it around, avoid the question.

Abi   Dannielle . . .

Danni   Ask me what I'm talking about. Why can't you do that?

Abi   Right, thass . . .

Danni (*pre-empting*)   Thass it . . .

Abi   I'm . . .

Danni   . . . I'm done . . .

Abi   I'm not going to say . . .

Danni   . . . say anymore!

Danni *goes inside.*

Abi   Damn it!

Masie   I know how you feel girl.

Abi   Don't say that.

Masie   I begged him and I begged him, until I couldn't speak, not to go with his friends, cos deep down I knew he wasn't coming back.

Abi   Oh Lord.

Masie   I know how you feel.

Abi   I'm at my wits' end with the pair of them, you lost your only boy, how can you be so calm?

Masie   Abigail, when was the last time you really thought about home?

Abi   What?

Masie   The truth now.

Abi   Why?

Masie   Come on tell me.

Abi   A few days ago when I got your letter. I was out here, and we, us. . .

Masie   Us?

Abi   It's crazy, it's like I saw the team playing. There was you, me, Jenny, Cita, everybody. I think we were winning.

Masie   You think?

Abi   I scored a six and then. . .

Masie   Wat, come on, wat?

Abi   She turned around.

Masie   Who?

Abi   Me. It was like I was looking right at myself.

Masie   Darling the same thing happened to me, well almost. It's not crazy at all. Abi I swear to you at the funeral reception, I shut my eyes for a minute, when I opened them, I found myself standing right in the middle of Lambert Street.

Abi   Lambert Street!

Masie   I swear to God. I saw my house. You remember that time I was stayin' with Uncle Ed. I saw myself climbing outta the window, Uncle Ed must have been drunk again. I walked right up the street to your house. You were sitting on the porch crying cos Miss Tyler had upset you again, I wanted to put my arms around you, then he pulled me.

Abi   Who?

Masie   Ferdy! Always spoiling my fun, he woke me up.

Abi   There you see, you musta bin dreaming.

Masie   But I tell you it was real. I was there. And the feeling I had, oh God, Abi it was like happiness itself was giving me one huge cuddle. I've never felt that good, I was so angry wid him, day and night since, I wanted to go back.

Abi   So why haven't you?

Masie   Because I need your help.

Abi   Help?

Masie   Your one was just as strong as mine, perhaps stronger, we can both go back.

Abi   And do what?

Masie   I don't know. Let's do all the worrying when we get there.

Abi   No, let's go and put you to bed.

Masie   I'm not joking here. I think we can do it, I know we can.

Abi   Masie stop talking stupidness.

Masie   You wanted to know wat can make me feel better, well this can, just do it.

Abi   Oh come on Masie . . .

Masie (*pleading*)   Abi . . .

Abi   Now stop that. That doesn't work anymore.

Masie   If it doesn't work, put me to bed, call the doctor, let him carry me out in a straightjacket, just do it, please, please.

Abi   Alright, alright. So what now?

Masie   Thank you darling. Take my hand in yours, close your eyes, now think and I mean really think. Ya thinkin'?

Abi   I'm thinkin'.

Masie   What do you see?

Abi   You. I'm sitting below your bedroom window, waiting for you to come out. Your Uncle Ed is calling after you, but we run on through Lambert Street. We nearly knock over Miss Stuart, she says summin.

Masie   What?

Abi   I don't know, but I think it's to you.

Masie   Keep thinking Abi.

Abi   What d'you think I'm doing?

Masie   Harder now.

Abi   Alright, I see . . .

Masie   Who, who?

Abi   Miss Tyler, I'm pretending I can't hear her.

Masie (*smiling*)   Good girl, who else?

Abi   There's us, I see Lambert's Field, our cricket field.

At this point **Masie** *opens her eyes. She slowly removes her hands from* **Abi**, *who does not notice. Lights rise slowly on the cricket field. Two young girls,* **Jenny** *and* **Cita**, *are playing.*

Masie   What else?

Abi   Oh my god, I see Jenny, Cita, Paula. Thelma and Naomi have just showed up on their bikes, the team, I can see the whole team.

Abi *can feel that* **Masie** *is not there. She opens her eyes. She is surprised to find herself standing on the field. She gets up to join* **Abi**.

Masie   Look girl, look where we are, what did I tell you?

Abi   No, no. Everything seems so real. How Masie?

Masie   We wished, it happened, who cares about the in-between? Not me darling. You scared?

Abi   Yes.

Masie   Don't be.

They watch as a young black girl, **Shirley***, enters, she looks around.*

Masie   Recognise her?

Abi   No, wait a minute, that ain't . . .

Masie/Abi   Insect Shirley! (*They laugh.*)

Masie   She never used the brains God gave her.

Abi   I thought you two were friends.

Masie   Only cos she married my fool of a cousin.

Abi   Still no way to talk about her.

Masie *takes off her shoes and runs over.*

Abi   Masie, don't, Masie . . .

Masie   You alright girl, you look lost.

Abi   Don't.

Shirley   I want to join the club.

Masie   They soon come.

Shirley   I know, thank you.

Abi *pulls her back over.*

Abi   Wat do you think you're doing?

Masie   Just talkin'.

Abi   Well don't.

Masie   You worry too much, just accept it, you'll feel better I promise.

Abi   How would you know?

More of the girls' team enter, including **Young Abi** *and* **Young Masie**. **Masie** *points them out.*

Masie   Now who do you think they are?

Abi   Masie stop this, you hear me, stop it! Wat you tryin' to do, drive me mad?

Masie   Just look at us.

Young Masie   Name?

Shirley   Wat?

Young Masie   Your name!

Shirley   Shirley Hamilton.

Young Abi   Your age?

Shirley   Fifteen.

Young Masie   Address?

Shirley   My wat? . . . You bin to my house plenty of times, come on Masie, you want me in the team or not.

Young Abi   Go practise wid Jenny and Cita, we're gonna have a game in a minute.

The girls giggle. **Masie** *laughs also.*

Masie   What were we like? Abi will you come on, this is not my doing.

Abi   And my arse is blue. Stop this now you hear me?

Masie   You better keep your voice down.

Abi   I will not.

Masie   They are looking at us.

Abi   No.

Masie   They're coming over.

Abi   No!

Young Masie   Morning Miss May.

Masie   Morning girls.

Abi   Miss May?

Masie   How you doing sweetiepie?

Young Masie   Oh I'm fine.

Masie   You got quite a team here.

Young Masie   We need them. Got a game coming up real soon.

Masie   Clanton Street.

Young Masie   You know about that?

Masie   Word gets around.

Young Masie   We're gonna beat them good.

Masie   I know you will. (*She feels* **Abi***'s glare.*) You will!

Young Masie (*to* **Abi**)   Masie Williams.

Abi (*nervous*)   Pleased to meet you.

Young Abi   Abigail Sandford.

Abi   Abi . . . Miss Carter.

Masie   Well shake hands nuh?

Abi *is terrified, they shake hands but* **Young Abi** *is reluctant to let go.*

Young Abi   I know you, don't I?

Abi No we haven't met.

Young Abi Yeah we have.

Abi I said no!

Young Abi Alright.

Masie Masie, you bin practising that move wid the ball I taught you?

Young Masie Oh yes, come let me show you.

Abi Wait I wan' to talk to you Miss May!

Masie Later yeah.

Abi Now!

Masie Later.

They go off, leaving the two **Abi***s alone.*

Young Masie (*offstage*) Team, come. You too Insect Shirley.

The girls laugh as they exit as well.

Young Abi Don't worry, Masie does that to me all the time. She never listens to a word I say.

Abi This is crazy.

Young Abi Wat you say?

Abi Nothing.

Young Abi Please don't bite off my head again, but I do know you. Did you know my mother, Gloria Sandford?

Abi No! Yes, I knew your mother.

Young Abi She died last year you know.

Abi I'm sorry.

Young Abi It's alright. So you want to practise with me?

Abi Oh no dear, I'm not that good.

Young Abi   Come on, I bet you're wicked like Miss May.

Abi   She bin teachin' you then?

Young Abi   Oh yes, mostly Masie though, them two are like that, everytime she comes.

Abi   When did you first meet her?

Young Abi   A few months back. I didn't like her at first, she fills Masie's head with a lot of nonsense.

Abi   Like what?

Young Abi   The club. Sayin' we're gonna play forever, be famous around the world. Masie laps it all up.

Abi   She's a dreamer.

Young Abi   You know.

They catch each other's eyes.

Abi   You remind me of someone I used to know.

Young Abi   Did she play?

Abi   Oh yes.

Young Abi   Any good?

Abi   The best.

Young Abi   Well, no more cricket for me. My daddy's coming back this weekend. Gotta persuade him to stay here, instead of working up in the country, going to show him I'm a good girl. Miss Tyler will have to leave me alone, you know Miss Tyler?

Abi   Oh yes I know her.

Young Abi   Tell me something. Did she have black teeth even when she was little?

Abi   Abigail!

Young Abi   Sorry shouldn't have said that.

Abi Yes, she did actually. (*They laugh.*)

Young Abi I'm gonna be a nurse.

Abi Thass nice, but your daddy will have summin to say about that.

Young Abi No he won't. He's gonna be proud.

Abi Why are you telling me all this?

Young Abi Daddy always taught me to be a friend to everyone I meet, didn't you know I'm a country girl!

Abi (*laughs*) Of course! Forget about your daddy for a minute, why are you telling me this?

Young Abi Because . . .

Abi I think you should play.

Young Abi Why?

Abi You just should.

Young Abi But my plans?

Abi Plans don't work out.

Young Abi Sure they will. Listen right, my dream's this . . .

Abi Don't say another word to me about it. This has gone on far enough.

Young Abi What has?

Abi Forget you ever saw me Abi alright, enjoy your family, enjoy your gift from your father . . .

Young Abi Who are you?

Abi Miss May, Miss May!

Young Abi Wait, who are you? Tell me.

Abi I'm so sorry.

Young Abi For what?

Abi   Everything . . . nothing!

The two **Masie***s arrive.*

Abi   We are leaving.

Masie   Abi . . .

Abi   Right now!

Young Abi   No, answer my question.

Young Masie   Come Abi, leave them alone.

Young Abi   Let me go Masie. (*To* **Abi**.) I want to know who you are.

Abi   We're leaving.

Young Masie   Come on Abi.

Young Abi   Lemme go.

Young Masie   You wan' me to punch you out?

Young Abi   Try it!

Abi *refuses to look at her younger self.*

Young Abi (*to* **Young Masie**)   Move from me!

She runs off.

Abi   I want to go.

Masie   What happened?

Abi   She was going on and on about her father.

Masie   And that wasn't telling you something?

Abi   No!

Masie   I don't believe you.

Abi   I don't care.

Masie   Abigail, don't you see this is for you as well as for me. It's not your fault your mother died.

Abi   Shut up about that.

Masie   No! She caught you sneaking off school with me, she was giving you the beating of your life, you prayed for her to stop.

Abi   Then she died, right in front of me.

Masie   You know she had a bad heart.

Abi   No Masie no! You're a damn liar. You've bin here before, Lord knows how many times.

Masie   Alright yes.

Abi   How? What is going on?

Masie   What does it matter? There's a lot of pain inside you girl.

Abi   There is nothing inside of me.

Masie   So you've forgiven your father for abandoning you?

Abi   Why are you doing this to me?

Masie   Forget about all of them. Look over there, Jenny Vincent, she's bin married for thirty odd years, working as a cleaner in some office can never afford to buy her own home. Connie Phillips, still hanging around Lambert Street looking for a man, any man at her age.

Abi   I know about Jenny and Connie.

Masie   Then you must know if you had stayed in the team we would never have lost that game against the Clanton boys.

Abi   Oh Masie. You really believe me scoring some sixes would have changed our lives? Come off it.

Masie   Susie Tanner, Maggie Gordon, Shirley Hamilton, after that game they all scatter to the winds. Look what happened to them, look what happened to you.

Abi   No. I don't know how you did it and I don't care.

Masie   Look me in the eye and tell me you don't want this.

Abi   I don't want it.

Masie   You disappoint me.

Abi   I'm going back. You hear me? I said . . .

Masie   Alright fine!

Act Two

Scene One

London, early morning, three days later. **Abi** *is watering her plants. She is quietly singing to herself.* **Danni** *enters from the house carrying her hold-all.*

Danni   What you doing up so early?

Abi   The only time I can see you these days. No breakfast again? You should always make time to eat in the mornings sweetheart.

Danni   I'm gonna miss my bus.

Abi   Oh to hell with the bus, miss college for the day.

Danni   And muck up my exams? Can't have that Mum.

Abi   Look child I know it's not the first time you've missed college. So you can make time for me. What's all this business with Shanelle?

Danni   What business?

Abi   Come on.

Danni   Come on what?

Abi   Why are you doing this.

Danni   Oh Mum don't talk like that.

Abi   Like what?

Danni   Like you're begging. It's no wonder they laugh at you.

Abi   Well pardon me.

Danni   I do thass the problem. If you knew I was bunking off college, how come you didn't say nuttin?

Abi   What, me sticking my nose into your affairs, showing you up? Can't have that Danni.

Danni   It would have been something.

Abi   You never want me to help you, never. Remember that time when you were four, and you wanted to sew a button on your dress all by yourself? 'I can do it Mum, I can do it.' Dannielle I am not a mindreader. How am I supposed to know?

Danni   Why did you let Michael back in?

Abi   Not the damn room again.

Danni   I'm fed up, every time him and Judith split up, it's always the same.

Abi   We have an agreement, he promised there'll be no trouble this time.

Danni   Yeah right.

Abi   What am I supposed to do, fling him out on the street?

Danni   We're not talking car radios and mobile phones Mum. You know what's getting into now, don't you? But you just stand there doing nuttin.

Abi   Oh stop your noise.

Danni   I wouldn't get as many bruises.

Abi   Don't use Michael as an excuse for your fighting, it's she. (*Pointing over to next door.*) That mouth on legs.

Danni   That's right blame Faye.

Abi   Well you want to blame Michael.

Danni   Stop hiding will you?

Abi   I'm not hiding. I am fed up with everyone trying to climb inside my head.

Danni   What the hell are you talking about?

Abi   You're rude you know.

Danni   And you only care about yourself.

Abi   And you only care about having your dinner on the table.

Danni   Mum you can't even cook properly.

Abi (*outraged*)   What! (*Throwing her hold-all.*) Go and get your bus Danni now!

Danni   Right!

Danni *leaves.*

Abi (*back to watering the plants*)   Can't cook, can't cook? Yes you look like you're starving.

Masie *enters, she sees* **Abi** *and goes to walk back in.*

Abi   Where you going Masie?

Masie   For a walk.

Abi   Another one? Wat is it about here you find so fascinating? Twenty-odd years I've been living here, and I still hate the damn place.

Masie   So move.

Abi   And go where? Are you still vex with me?

Masie   You didn't even try to like it.

Abi   Masie Williams you never know when to stop. There she was, fifteen years old, planning out her whole life, talking about her father. I don't need to hear that.

Masie   What were you and Danni fighting about?

Abi   The generation gap, and all that's in it.

Masie   You should have made her play.

Abi   Danni?

Masie   No, you, her, Abi!

Abi   You're wrong.

Masie   Trust me, watch all your problems go away.

Abi   Oh Masie I can't. Where are you going?

Masie   Nowhere! (*She stops.*) Want some tea?

Abi   Yeah I would love some.

Masie *goes back in.* **Abi** *clocks* **Faye** *coming out.*

Faye   Yes?

Abi   Wat you bin doin' to my daughter?

Faye   I ain't done nuttin to her.

Abi   You keep on dragging her into trouble, leave her alone you hear me? Worry about yourself for a change.

Faye   Myself?

Abi   You call yourself a mother? You're a disgrace.

Faye   Don't talk like you know me, you're not my mum, you not my mum, you got no right.

Abi   I work for a living, I've got plenty right to . . .

Faye   No not while your precious little boy is feeding half the crackheads around here with shit you don't.

Abi   What you saying?

Faye   Oh yeah, right. Like you know nothing. You say I'm a disgrace.

Abi   You little bitch.

Faye   Fuck off. (*Goes in.*)

Abi   I control my house, my kids. You hear me!

She stops and holds her head in her hands. **Ferdy**, **Masie**'s *husband, leans over the gate.*

Ferdy   Psst. Excuse me madam, but you wouldn't mind telling me where I might find a couple of exciting women for some morning fun eh?

Abi   Well here is one, come, let me take a good look at you.

Ferdy *enters the garden, they laugh.*

Ferdy   How's my girl?

Abi   Ferdy Watson get yourself over here. (*They embrace.*) It's about time.

Ferdy   Hey, traffic was a bitch you know.

Abi   How you feeling?

Ferdy   Oh fine, fine.

Abi   Vanessa, Claudia?

Ferdy   Coping, better than we. Hey hey hold on, girl you bin crying. Is who upset my Abigail? Tell me now.

Abi   Enough of your hard man act. Worry about your wife.

Ferdy   Where is she?

Abi   She soon come. You bring the pictures I asked you.

Ferdy (*hands them over*)   Here.

Abi   Oh, she is beautiful.

Ferdy   Course, takes after her grandpa.

Abi   Oh hush.

Ferdy   Look at the next one.

Abi   Oh Lord.

Ferdy (*giggling*)   Thass my favourite one.

Abi   Who put that hat on the poor little thing?

Ferdy   Vanessa, the little scamp.

Abi I wonder who she get that from?

Ferdy (*innocent*) Me?

Abi You!

Masie *enters carrying two mugs.*

Ferdy How's my favourite girl?

Masie What are you doing here?

Ferdy I've come to see you of course. Didn't Abi say I was coming?

Masie (*to* **Abi**) And you moan to me about interfering with your life.

Ferdy What she say?

Abi Nothing.

Ferdy Let me help you wid that.

Masie I can do it.

Ferdy OK. Oh Tea. That's nice.

Masie Good one Ferdy.

Abi I'll go inside and make you some.

Masie You do that Abigail.

Ferdy You know I wouldn't mind summin a little stronger.

Abi Alright, one black coffee.

Ferdy (*pretending to be glad.*) Nice.

Abi *goes.*

Masie Summin a little stronger, you're driving aren't you?

Ferdy Yeah but . . .

Masie But? You expect me to drive you home rat-arsed again.

Ferdy   No.

Masie   Yes.

Ferdy   What kind of greeting is this? I've just come to see you, you're my wife remember. So how are you, you alright?

Masie   Yes!

Ferdy   Everyone bin askin' at the church for you, especially the Reverend.

Masie   Thass nice.

Ferdy   Vanessa passed her exams.

Masie   Don't do this.

Ferdy   Do what?

Masie   Don't go around the block like you always do, what do you want?

Ferdy   Of all the stupid . . . you know wat I want, you to come home. You're not the only one who loved him.

Masie   You think that's what it's all about, you're a blind man Ferdy.

Ferdy   Well tell me then.

Masie   I don't have the time.

Ferdy   Masie . . .

Masie   Just go back to your fancy woman and leave me alone.

Ferdy   How many more times do I have to tell you? Lena is not my fancy woman. We were just talkin' and ting . . .

Masie   Did you show her?

Ferdy   Show her what?

Masie   Your ting?

Ferdy   Don't get nasty alright. Nothing happened.

Masie   What kinda fool do you think I am? Thirty-odd
years of marriage Ferdy and you think I don't recognise the
'I hope Masie doesn't find out' face? You're wearing it now
sweetheart. It was embarrassing enough when you were our
son's age, now it's just boring and pathetic.

Ferdy   He has a name you know, our son.

Masie   I know.

Ferdy   Then use it! We had a son named Jeffrey. You still
blame me don't you?

Masie   You could've stopped him, he would have listened
to you.

Ferdy   Them white boys were nothing but trash.

Masie   You should have stopped him.

Ferdy   Why, I'm proud of what he did!

Masie   Proud? Proud he's dead? He should have gone to
the police.

Ferdy   What century you living in woman? It's our war,
we fight it ourselves.

Masie   Shut up, shut up, save that rubbish for the ones
who believe it. (*Mocking him.*) Fight the war ourselves, you
bin sniffing Vanessa's Tipp-Ex?

Ferdy   You're wrong.

Masie   Course I am. I'm always wrong. Like I was wrong
putting him in that school, five miles from where we lived, I
was wrong not letting his friends come into our home, I was
wrong when I yelled at him for losing the best job he ever
had, like I was wrong on the night he . . . Yes Ferdy I'm
always wrong.

Ferdy   We can't go on like this. I can't keep lying to
Vanessa. She ain't stupid you know, Claudia is worried too.

Masie   That makes a change. I suppose as usual you that went to see her. Knew it. She's too good for us now ain't it?

Ferdy   Will you please come home?

Masie   You know when I held him in my arms for the first time, it was the only real time I believed I could bury what I left behind, I remember whispering to his ear, I will protect you forever my sweet, but later I could see in his eyes, him plotting to get what he could out of me.

Ferdy   Stop this talk.

Masie   You whisked him away, outta my arms, moulded him into your image, you moulded all of them. I told him I'd protect him, you made a liar out of me. Well to hell with you, Claudia, the baby, Vanessa, Jeffrey!

Ferdy   I don't believe you said that.

Masie   Then I'll say it again. To hell with Jeffrey!

Ferdy   Don't! We need you.

Masie   I need you to get out of my sight.

Ferdy   You want a doctor.

Masie   And why is that?

Ferdy   Abi was sayin' how you bin daydreaming again.

Masie   That girl tell more lies than me. Ferdy will you please go?

Ferdy   You coming home or not? Last chance.

Masie   Wat have I told you about your macho act, it don't work on me. But don't worry my love, I'm coming home, but not to Streatham.

Ferdy   What you sayin' now?

Masie   Nothing.

Ferdy   Masie . . .

Masie   Leave me alone!

Scene Two

The same location, one hour later. **Abi** *is outside knitting. Sound of furniture being smashed around.* **Abi** *jumps. She stops what she is doing and waits nervously.* **Michael** *steams outside.*

Michael   Mum have you bin in my room? Have you bin in my room? What have I told you about that?

Abi   This is still my house.

Michael   Mum where are they? Where are they?

Abi   You're dealing drugs!

Michael   Don't tell me my business.

Abi   My God what have I done?

Michael   Just gimme them.

Abi   Why Michael?

Michael   Mum gimme them.

Abi   Why are you punishing me?

Michael   What? You're bloody mad.

Abi   You want to hear me beg you?

Michael   Look I ain't got time for this, not today.

Abi   Is this why Judith won't let you see Patrick?

Michael   Forget about Patrick, Mum.

Abi   I'm asking you a question.

Michael   Shut up and listen for once, forget about Patrick. He ain't coming round no more.

Abi   Why is that?

Michael   The stuff Mum.

Abi   Answer my question.

Michael   She's got herself a new man.

Abi   So?

Michael   So he wears a suit to work, and Patrick adores him.

Abi   You're still his father.

Michael   Not no more. He's got himself a new daddy.

Abi   That's not right at all.

Michael   So what would you prefer then, him coming round and you knowing what you know? That don't make you a very good grandma.

Abi   You think you can push every girl around like you do me. I warned you. How the hell can Patrick look up to you when . . . ?

Michael   It's always him isn't it!

Abi   You are a disgrace!

Michael   What is this huh? We're Sandfords Mum, we don't care about anything. You taught me well.

Abi   He will always be your son.

Michael   The boy's well out of it.

Abi   That isn't true. Listen to me . . .

Michael   No, tell me where did you hide them? Don't make me tear this place apart Mum please.

Abi   I flushed them.

Michael   No, no you didn't.

Abi   Oh yes.

Michael   No, no! No. You got any idea how much they're worth, any idea, Jesus! (*Swings his arm around, accidently hitting* **Abi**.) Mum, Mum, I'm sorry.

Abi   It's alright, leave me.

Michael   If I hit you for real, you wouldn't stand up.

Abi   I have knitting to do.

Michael   It was an accident.

Abi   Making Danni a sweater, make up for her birthday.

Michael   You know where it's going to end up, in the bin.
You know Danni likes to get her own clothes, but you still
do it, nothing sinks in. Wat am I talkin' to you for? You
don't know how to. You're nuttin without Dad. All you do is
go on about sweet Jamaica. Even when Dad was here you
did the same, he gave up plenty too you know. All you did
was make a fool of him. You wanna talk about fools. All I
see is some sad old woman, and she ain't much. (**Michael**
exits.)

Abi *tries to carry on knitting; she gives up and throws it to the floor.*
Masie *comes out.*

Abi   Masie?

Masie   I'm not talking to you.

Abi   I had to do something.

Masie   You didn't have to go behind my back.

Abi   Talk to me please.

Masie   About wat?

Abi   Anything.

Masie   I haven' got time alright, I'll do it on my own . . .
(*Notices* **Abi**'s *lip.*) Wat happened to you, let me see Abi,
Michael do this, are things this bad?

Abi   He didn't mean it, at least I think . . . Oh Masie I
wish I could just trade it all in you know; job, home,
children the lot. I've got nothing left to give them. You
know when Teddy died, I thought 'I'm free'. When I was
alone in my bedroom I threw all of his things off the
dressing table and our wedding picture right across the
room. Already my head was filling up with ideas of going
back home, study to be a nurse, Miss Tyler was dead,

Daddy was gone, I was free, but soon as I turned around I saw little Michael by the door, and girl the look in his eyes, I'm a walking, talking curse.

Masie   No you're not.

Abi   But he came looking for me, I should have put my arm around him, wiped his tears, I'm his mother. I haven't done much of a job, for either of them.

Masie   Listen girl you are no curse. You are Abigail Sandford, devil with a bat. You couldn't be a curse to anyone.

Abi   You always see the best in me Masie Williams.

Masie   Someone has to.

Abi   I don't want to lose you.

Masie   Who says you do?

Abi   Oh Masie, is this what it feels like?

Masie   What?

Abi   Losing our minds?

Masie   Do you think we have?

Abi   It seemed real to me.

Masie   So what are you saying?

Abi   You want some company?

Masie   Well this is a turnaround. Take my hand in yours, close your eyes, now think.

Abi   I'm thinking.

Scene Three

The cricket field, Kingston. The match is in full swing. **Young Masie** *is watching; she is the only one taking an interest in the game.* **Jenny** *and* **Shirley** *are sitting alongside her.*

Young Masie (*calling out*)   Watch the ball now Cita, hit it y' hearing me? Me say hit it! Now run girl!

Jenny   John Wayne! Girl shut your mout, Audie Murphy is the best cowboy that ever lived.

Shirley   Could he fight like John Wayne, draw up his six shooter like John Wayne can? No.

Jenny   Shirley I'm only gonna say one thing to you right, in one film I see Audie Murphy shoot down train robbers, become sheriff, and wipe out a tribe of dem nasty apache!

Shirley   Wat movie?

Jenny   I don't remember.

Shirley   G'way!

Young Masie   You two here to play or not? Jenny you're up next, be ready.

Shirley   Wass the point, they're beating us good you know.

Young Masie   We can still win this, I don't want to hear dem say . . . girls can't play, you hear me.

Clanton Street Boys (*offstage*)   Howzat!

Shirley   Masie we need a miracle.

Jenny   We need Abi.

Masie   Just shut up!

Lights on **Abi**. **Young Masie** *and the girls freeze.* **Abi** *is holding her shoes, she looks very happy as she sings to herself.*

Abi   Masie and I spent ages visiting our old haunts, that
sorta thing. All the way down Lambert Street we went; we
saw Miss Stuart still sitting on her stool on the corner,
(*laughs*) the Brewster boys, Masie's house, my house. It
hadn't changed a bit, every door, every window looked
exactly the same. I never liked that place you know, it was
her house, Miss Tyler's! Staring at it made me remember
the day we first moved there. I was seven and we left the
country to live in Kingston, and I remember seeing this little
summin of a house perched on this hill. I say to myself 'I
have to walk up that (*tuts*) wid me only in sandals'. So I cried
blue murder to my daddy saying 'I don't want to go up
there!' Moma yelled 'Stop your foolishness!' But I cried and
I cried you see. Moma was rolling up her sleeves, ready to
give me a slap when Daddy turned round and say 'I'll tell
you what, you take my shoes and I take yours'. (*Laughs.*) So I
put his shoes on, and straight up the hill I went, Mummy of
course thought we were playing the arse of ourselves, but we
just laughed, couldn't stop. Oh, sweet Jamaica. (*Puts her arms
around herself, giving herself a cuddle.*) Masie was right. I feel,
reunited wid my soul. (*Laughs.*) 'Hello soul, hello Abi. Long
time no hear girl!' Long time.

Masie *comes up behind* **Abi**.

Masie   Talkin' to yourself, people will think you're mad
girl.

Abi   Oh hush. You know Masie you're right. Why in
God's name did we ever want to leave?

Masie   We got work to do. Come on!

Abi   Come on!

Clanton Street Boys (*offstage*)   Out!

Abi *and* **Masie** *go over to where the game is playing.* **Jenny** *goes
out to bat.* **Cita** *joins the girls.*

Young Masie   Watch the ball, you hear me Jenny? Just
hit the ball.

Jenny   I hear you.

Cita   See that boy bowling, im nice.

Young Masie   You here to play or not?

Cita   Ease up nah!

Young Masie   Hey! Just don't say a word to me.

Shirley   Can I go to the toilet please?

Young Masie   Just get outta my sight. Damn you Abi!

Masie *stares at her friend.* **Abi** *feels uncomfortable.*

Masie (*to* **Young Masie**)   Hey girl!

Young Masie   Oh hi Miss May. (*Sound of a ball being hit.*) Go Jenny!

Masie   How you doing?

Young Masie   Can't you tell?

Masie   You miss Abi don't you?

Young Masie (*to* **Abi**)   Wat did you say to her?

Abi   Me?

Young Masie   She was fine before she spoke to you, fine.

Abi   I think you know it isn't true.

Young Masie   You know wat's gonna happen here,we'll lose, then I'll lose them.

Masie   Listen to me girl, listen. It's not going to happen, you gotta wish hard. You hear me? Now come on, you can still win this. Right Miss C?

Clanton Street Boys (*offstage*)   Howzat!

Young Masie   Shirley you're up, Shirley! I suppose it's down to me.

Masie   Just keep them busy. Whack the ball straight over Kingston.

Young Masie   I'll do my best. (*She goes.*)

Abi   Why are you looking at me like that Masie?

Masie   You know wat you have to do.

Abi   Why?

Masie   Why! Widowed, alone, raising two ungrateful pikne? One beats you, your own child.

Abi   Shut up.

Masie   You wouldn't be here if you didn't want this.

Abi   Masie listen.

Masie   No don't tell me you don't want this chance, just don't tell me that. Where you going?

Abi   Far away from you.

Masie   Good, that's good.

Abi   Just leave me alone.

Masie   You find her Abi, make her play.

Scene Four

Kingston. **Young Abi** *is sitting alone on the beach writing a letter.*

Young Abi   . . . and thank you for sending me the poetry book Daddy, it was lovely. I'm sorry as well that you couldn't come down that time, I know you're busy. I really miss you though. I hope you're looking after yourself or I'll have to come up there. So from now on, no more foolishness from me. I'll get on wid school, get married – you best keep yourself fit cos you're gonna get plenty grandchildren. No more of me thinking of myself, gonna make you happy Daddy. (**Abi** *enters at this point.*) Why aren't you here . . .

Young Abi/Abi   I want you here.

Young Abi *turns around quickly.*

Abi   It's only me.

Young Abi   How did you find me.

Abi   I knew you'd be here.

Young Abi   But how? No one knows, this is where I . . .

Abi   Write letters to your Daddy.

Young Abi   You know too much about me.

Abi   Doesn't that tell you something?

Young Abi   If it did would I be askin'?

Abi *laughs.*

Young Abi   Wat, stop that, wat?

Abi   Still got an answer for everything. How I've missed that.

Young Abi   You're no friend of my mother's.

Abi   Correct.

Young Abi   So who are you?

Abi   The team are getting well beat you know.

Young Abi   That's not my problem anymore.

Abi   Sweetheart I know wat you're going through, but turning your back on your friends won't help you believe me.

Young Abi   Believe you?

Abi   Abi listen, we don't have much time.

Young Abi   I'm not going to listen to you.

Abi   Look at your letter, look at it. (*Reciting.*) 'Dear Daddy, I've got some good news for you. I've finally left that stupid ol' cricket team.'

Young Abi *screws up the letter and steps away, terrified.*

Young Abi   You get away from me.

Abi (*still reciting*)   I've decided that you and Miss Tyler were right all along.

Young Abi   You're a damn crazy woman.

Abi   You just wait till you see me next. And thank you for sending me the poetry book Daddy, it was lovely.

Young Abi (*screams*)   Move from me!

Abi   . . . I'm sorry as well that you couldn't come down that time . . .

Abi *grabs the young girl's arm and rolls up her sleeve.*

Young Abi   Lemme go, you wan' me to punch you out?

Abi   Punch me? You got that scar on your arm when you were nine years old. Old man Rivers' dog bite you, right? (*Rolls up her sleeve.*) See?

Young Abi   No.

Abi   Look at me, look into my eyes, look!

Young Abi (*frantic.*)   No I say!

Young Abi *tries to run,* **Abi** *grabs her.*

Abi   Are you scared? Answer me, are you scared?

Young Abi   Yes.

Abi   Don't be.

Young Abi   I know, somehow I . . . (*Touches* **Abi**'s *scar on her arm but pulls away.*) How? I don't understand, how can you be here? Why are you here?

Abi   To escape, I wanted to see home again, to see you. I'm giving you a chance to change things.

Young Abi   What things?

Abi   Your life Abi.

Young Abi   How?

Abi   You musn't give up on yourself.

Young Abi   But I'm not going to, you must know that.

Abi   And you have to play the game.

Young Abi   Why? I know what I'm doing.

Abi   You don't. You only want what other people want you to have. Miss Tyler, your daddy . . .

Young Abi   No this ain't right at all, I'm gonna go University, I'm gonna . . .

Abi   That won't happen. Everything started from here Abi. Miss Tyler won't stop you know, she's gonna keep on making your life hell, an' you're so wrapped up in worrying after Daddy and working in her shop day and night. You'll be doing the right thing for everybody, Abigail, except yourself. Maybe if you had just carried on playing . . .

Young Abi   You're talking shit!

Abi   Abigail!

Young Abi   Wat, you never said shit before?

Abi   How much more proof do you want?

Young Abi   Plenty, about givin' up on myself.

Abi   You want to hear how I cried myself to sleep night after night cos Miss Tyler tell me Daddy don't love me? And shall I tell you how you really feel? You believe Daddy blames you for Moma's death.

Young Abi   Alright alright. Now tell me about my dream.

Abi (*laughs*)   Your dream.

Young Abi   My dream! The one that keeps me going, come on, alright, I can see myself when I'm older so happy, enjoying life and everything else around me. No Miss Tyler, nobody, there are times when I can't wait to get there, to be you, you bitch!

Abi What did you just say?

Young Abi You did it, didn't you, you gave up, that's why you're here.

Abi Don't speak that way to me.

Young Abi Yes, oh yes.

Abi I mean it.

Young Abi Tell me then.

Abi Things are different where I come from, pressure you wouldn't believe.

Young Abi You should have held on. So wat are you then. Not a nurse I take it. Come on, someone's cleaner, summin like that.

Abi No.

Young Abi You married? Children? To who, who?

Abi Teddy Carter.

Young Abi Oh Jesus! You mean to say I have pikne who look like him? What happened to my dream? How could you let this happen?

Abi We both did. I'm telling you. Soon Abi you won't even care. Four years from now you're gonna marry Teddy, believe it or not, right, he does grow to be a kind and decent man but you won't love him. Play the game. Hit some sixes, for you, Masie, the whole team. Abi please.

Young Abi Now I know who's really talkin'.

Abi (*impatient*) Me!

Young Abi Masie Williams. Not even that has changed, she still got you doing wat she wants. I thought you would have the strength to stand up to her by now.

Abi   But she's right about this.

Young Abi   You really think so?

Abi   Yes!

Young Abi   We are talkin' about the same Masie? The one who hid from Pearl Daniels in my backyard and begged me to beat up the girl? Or the one who always copies my homework? Listen I love Masie like a sister, but you really think she is doing this for us?

Abi   But I've never bin the same since I came to England. Day by day everything just went out of me. I can't even hit a ball now.

Young Abi   I can't believe you've forgotten so much. Who taught us how to play in the first place?

Abi   Big Charlie Bennett.

Young Abi   . . . Big Charlie Bennett. 'Now remember girl, hold the ball firmly in your palm, like so. An' when you bat, never take your eyes offa it, never.' When we moved from the country did we forget everything he taught us?

Abi   Of course not.

Young Abi   So why you forget now? You are Abigail Rosemary Sandford.

Abi   I know who I am.

Young Abi   Do you?

Young Abi *searches around the beach.*

Young Abi   There's always something. Ah!

Young Abi *finds some paper, rolls it up into a ball, and a piece of wood.*

Abi   What are you doing?

Young Abi   I'm going to bowl, you (*hands her the wood*) are going to bat.

Abi No I can't do this anymore. You're young.

Young Abi You're pathetic.

Abi You have been with me every day and night, what do you want me to say, I'm sorry?

Young Abi Don't be sorry, hit the ball.

Young Abi *bowls,* **Abi** *misses it completely.* **Young Abi** *says nothing when getting the ball of paper back.*

Young Abi Again.

Abi We are wasting time.

Young Abi Again.

Abi It should be you. Come on Abi.

Young Abi You see me? This Abigail Sandford would never give up. I know who I am, I don't know you. I hate you.

Abi Then you must hate yourself.

Young Abi You best hit this damn ball.

Abi *(fierce)* Alright!

Abi *catches the ball with the bat and whacks the ball clean over. She feels something.*

Abi Did I just do that?

Young Abi Yes! You see, you see.

Abi But Jesus Christ.

Young Abi You never lose a gift like that.

Abi But Jesus Christ!

Young Abi How does the dream look now? (**Abi** *is beaming.*) I love that smile.

Abi Throw me another one, I gotta tell myself that was no fluke.

Young Abi   That was no fluke. (*Taking the piece of wood from her.*) And I think you know. (*Laughs.*)

Abi   What?

Young Abi   Teddy Carter?

Abi   Worry about your children, I tell you Dannielle and Michael . . .

Young Abi   No, don't say anymore.

Abi   Wat about the team, Masie?

Young Abi   They'll just have to learn, like we? Masie won't like that.

Abi   Nor will Miss May.

Young Abi   Yours? You mean to say, Miss May is . . .

Abi   Yes.

Young Abi   Should have known.

Abi   You think your Masie knows?

Young Abi   She's keeping it a secret if she does. Wouldn't surprise me.

Abi   Will you just listen to one thing I tell you?

Young Abi   One thing.

Abi   It wasn't your fault Moma died. You didn't cause the fire. No matter what that witch Miss Tyler says. You must believe that.

Young Abi   Do you?

Abi   Yes, I think I do now.

Young Abi   Then we don't have a problem.

Abi   Where did you learn to be so smart?

Young Abi   Didn't you know . . .

Abi/Young Abi   I'm a country girl! (*They laugh, then embrace.*)

Abi   Oh sweetheart. Come with me.

Young Abi   No, I'll stay here.

Abi   Abigail Sandford does not hide you know.

Young Abi   I'm not hiding from anything.

Abi   So come with me.

Abi *takes the hand of* **Young Abi**. *They stroll off.*

Scene Five

The cricket field, Kingston. **Young Masie** *stands alone. Sound of* **Clanton Street Boys** *laughing and singing.*

Young Masie   Shut up!

Boy   Wha' wrong wid you, can't take losin'?

Young Masie   I can take a lot of things like a stick into the back of your blasted neck!

The **Clanton Street Boys** *laugh and cheer louder, their voices fade away.* **Young Abi** *and* **Abi** *enter.*

Young Masie   So you finally show up then?

Young Abi   Masie . . .

Young Masie   No.

Young Abi   Let me talk to you.

Young Masie   I said leave me!

Young Masie *runs off,* **Young Abi** *goes after her.* **Masie** *enters from the other side.*

Abi   It's over.

Masie   You think I don't know that? You think I was
going to stay and watch it happen all over again?

Abi   Let me talk to you.

Masie   We had this conversation before you know, I can
see them from here look; you're putting your arm around
me telling me why you did it, how your family is so
important to you, how we still got time. You were so good I
started to believe it. Abi, don't you realise for people like us,
there are fewer days ahead than there are behind? You
couldn't persuade her, maybe I can.

Abi   Leave her alone.

Masie   Afraid I'll change her mind?

Abi   You're wasting your time, cos if you're talkin' to her,
you're talkin' to me.

Masie   Still thinkin' the world will wait for you Mrs
Abigail Carter! You can't even see that same world is
pushing you into the ground.

Abi   But not you?

Masie   No not me!

Abi   Enough of this. You have a family and they need you.

Masie   What I have is an empty house, and you want me
to give up all this again? Who am I Abi – that young feisty
go-getter of a girl? I loved those things about me, I miss
those things.

Abi   You don't have to, they're right there!

Masie   Or am I some sad old woman who lives to bore
her kids, the one they just humour and patronise when they
think I'm just rambling on about foolishness? They think we
don't know, but we do, don't we?

Abi   Yes.

Masie   You can do wat you want.

Abi   Masie . . .

Masie   Don't worry I won't trouble her, but that is me over there, she needs me.

Abi   You'll fail.

Masie   Then very little would have been lost.

Abi   Don't say that.

Masie   Go home Abi.

Abi   I'm not going to leave you here.

Masie   Fine, stay. (**Abi** *reaches out to touch her,* **Masie** *pushes her away.*) No, I let you put your arm around me before. Just go. And Abi, you know if you can ever afford to come home and go to the cricket field, you might see a very, very old woman waving a bat. You never know girl.

Abi   Gimme your hand Masie.

Masie   No.

Abi   You are coming home with me.

Masie   No.

Abi *grabs her, they struggle, hard.*

Masie   Abi let me go. Come on now. You wan' me to punch you out?

Abi   Try it.

Masie *breaks free.*

Masie   Keep an eye on the kids for me. Bye my darling. (*She runs.*)

Abi (*screaming*)   Masie!

Scene Six

London, the next morning. Sound of a baby crying, **Faye** *comes out, she lights up a cigarette.*

Faye   Oh shut up, please, just shut up.

Faye *is distracted by loud sounds coming from next door. She looks over and sees* **Abi** *dragging a packed suitcase out. They clock each other.*

Faye (*laughs*)   Fuck . . .

Abi   Yes!

Danni (*coming out*)   Mum, what you doing?

Abi   Out of my way child.

Danni   Tell me what you're doing first.

Abi   Will you move?

Abi *goes inside.*

Faye   What's going on?

Danni   You asking me?

Abi *comes out dragging another bag.*

Danni   You're gonna do your back in dragging it like that.

Abi   Danni, Danni, leave me alone.

Danni   Mum will you slow down for a minute will ya? What are you doing with Michael's stuff? Is he moving out or something? Mum don't ignore me. Is Michael moving out?

Abi   Yes.

Danni   He told you?

Abi   No.

Danni   You chucking him out?

Abi   Yes child.

Danni   What for?

Abi   You're not stupid Dannielle.

Faye (*laughs*)   Sorry.

Abi   Go get the other box for me, go on.

Danni *goes.* **Abi** *goes over to* **Faye**.

Faye   Alright, come on, your insult for the day is . . .

Abi   You get my daughter into any more trouble, and I will cut in half every bone in your body.

Faye (*pretending to be aroused*)   Ooooh!

Abi   Yes. Go on, enjoy it. Because I'm telling you now it's gonna be for the last time.

Faye   What?

Abi   Tell that to everybody. (*Turns her back.*)

Faye   What? (*Baby cries.*) Alright, I'm coming.

Faye *goes back in.* **Danni** *comes out.*

Abi   Well put it down.

Danni   Don't you think it's a bit late for this, the assertive mother act?

Abi   No.

Michael *enters through the gate.*

Danni   Well don't tell me, show me.

Michael   What's going on, what are you doing with my things Mum?

Abi   It's not working out at all Michael.

Michael   What you talkin' about?

Abi   We had an agreement, you broke it. Now I've decided . . .

Michael   You've decided? Mum these are my things!

Abi   You need help.

Michael   Help for what? Mother I truly believe you've gone over the edge this time. You went in my room again, I can't believe you went in my room.

Abi   You're moving out.

Michael   Am I?

Abi   No one is going to laugh at me anymore.

Michael   Where are you getting this from please?

Abi   You're not that clever son.

Danni   That's what I told him.

Michael   Shut it.

Danni   No you shut it.

Michael   You want a slap?

Abi   Leave her alone!

Michael   Put my stuff back in my room, enough of this crap.

Abi   You promise to finish with that rubbish?

Michael   You flushed all I had down the bog.

Danni   You did that? Go Mum!

Abi   Alright Danni, quiet.

Michael   Are we finished now?

Abi   Do you promise me?

Michael   I ain't promising you shit!

Abi   Then you're going.

Michael   So what you saying Mum, you giving up on me, again?

Abi   Oh no, not this time Michael.

Michael (*laughs*)   Who you trying to fool Mum? Not me! (*Pointing at* **Danni**.) Go waste it on her. (*Grabs a box, heads back to the house.*)

Abi   I spoke to Judith this morning.

Michael   Judith! Mum Judith can fuck off . . .

Abi   Patrick's birthday next week.

Michael   So what?

Abi   She said to tell you . . .

Michael   You think I want to hear what she has to say . . .

Abi   She said to tell you, that she and David won't forget you're Patrick's father . . .

Michael   Yeah they say that now but . . .

Abi   . . . just as long as you don't! Don't you abandon him Michael.

Michael *tuts and walks back in.*

Danni *sighs. She picks up the other box.*

Abi   What are you doing? Put that down please.

Danni   He won't go Mum. He won't change.

Abi   I have.

Danni   What, you going to go through this every day?

Abi   If I have to.

Danni   You'll give up. You always do.

Abi   You really think so?

Abi *takes the box off her and tips it over.*

Danni   Alright, so what now?

Abi *laughs out loud.*

What?

Abi   How about a game of cricket?

Danni *goes back in, confused.* **Abi** *stands alone. She is still laughing. Lights up on the cricket field.* **Young Abi** *is with the team and is getting ready to bat. They both smile at each other just as* **Young Abi** *swings the bat and scores another six.*

End.

A SELECTED LIST OF
METHUEN MODERN PLAYS

☐	CLOSER	Patrick Marber	£6.99
☐	THE BEAUTY QUEEN OF LEENANE	Martin McDonagh	£6.99
☐	A SKULL IN CONNEMARA	Martin McDonagh	£6.99
☐	THE LONESOME WEST	Martin McDonagh	£6.99
☐	THE CRIPPLE OF INISHMAAN	Martin McDonagh	£6.99
☐	THE STEWARD OF CHRISTENDOM	Sebastian Barry	£6.99
☐	SHOPPING AND F***ING	Mark Ravenhill	£6.99
☐	FAUST (FAUST IS DEAD)	Mark Ravenhill	£5.99
☐	POLYGRAPH	Robert Lepage and Marie Brassard	£6.99
☐	BEAUTIFUL THING	Jonathan Harvey	£6.99
☐	MEMORY OF WATER & FIVE KINDS OF SILENCE	Shelagh Stephenson	£7.99
☐	WISHBONES	Lucinda Coxon	£6.99
☐	BONDAGERS & THE STRAW CHAIR	Sue Glover	£9.99
☐	SOME VOICES & PALE HORSE	Joe Penhall	£7.99
☐	KNIVES IN HENS	David Harrower	£6.99
☐	BOYS' LIFE & SEARCH AND DESTROY	Howard Korder	£8.99
☐	THE LIGHTS	Howard Korder	£6.99
☐	SERVING IT UP & A WEEK WITH TONY	David Eldridge	£8.99
☐	INSIDE TRADING	Malcolm Bradbury	£6.99
☐	MASTERCLASS	Terrence McNally	£5.99
☐	EUROPE & THE ARCHITECT	David Grieg	£7.99
☐	BLUE MURDER	Peter Nichols	£6.99
☐	BLASTED & PHAEDRA'S LOVE	Sarah Kane	£7.99

- All Methuen Drama books are available through mail order or from your local bookshop.

Please send cheque/eurocheque/postal order (sterling only) Access, Visa, Mastercard, Diners Card, Switch or Amex.

Expiry Date:_____ Signature: _____

Please allow 75 pence per book for post and packing U.K.
Overseas customers please allow £1.00 per copy for post and packing.

ALL ORDERS TO:

Methuen Books, Books by Post, TBS Limited, The Book Service, Colchester Road, Frating Green, Colchester, Essex CO7 7DW.

NAME: _____

ADDRESS: _____

_____

_____

Please allow 28 days for delivery. Please tick box if you do not wish to receive any additional information ☐

Prices and availability subject to change without notice.

METHUEN SCREENPLAYS

☐ BEAUTIFUL THING	Jonathan Harvey	£6.99
☐ THE ENGLISH PATIENT	Anthony Minghella	£7.99
☐ THE CRUCIBLE	Arthur Miller	£6.99
☐ THE WIND IN THE WILLOWS	Terry Jones	£7.99
☐ PERSUASION	Jane Austen, adapted by Nick Dear	£6.99
☐ TWELFTH NIGHT	Shakespeare, adapted by Trevor Nunn	£7.99
☐ THE KRAYS	Philip Ridley	£7.99
☐ THE AMERICAN DREAMS (THE REFLECTING SKIN & THE PASSION OF DARKLY NOON)	Philip Ridley	£8.99
☐ MRS BROWN	Jeremy Brock	£7.99
☐ THE GAMBLER	Dostoyevsky, adapted by Nick Dear	£7.99
☐ TROJAN EDDIE	Billy Roche	£7.99
☐ THE WINGS OF THE DOVE	Hossein Amini	£7.99
☐ THE ACID HOUSE TRILOGY	Irvine Welsh	£8.99
☐ THE LONG GOOD FRIDAY	Barrie Keeffe	£6.99
☐ SLING BLADE	Billy Bob Thornton	£7.99

• All Methuen Drama books are available through mail order or from your local bookshop.

Please send cheque/eurocheque/postal order (sterling only) Access, Visa, Mastercard, Diners Card, Switch or Amex.

☐☐☐☐☐☐☐☐☐☐☐☐☐☐☐☐

Expiry Date:_____ Signature: _____

Please allow 75 pence per book for post and packing U.K.
Overseas customers please allow £1.00 per copy for post and packing.

ALL ORDERS TO:

Methuen Books, Books by Post, TBS Limited, The Book Service, Colchester Road, Frating Green, Colchester, Essex CO7 7DW.

NAME: _____

ADDRESS: `_____

_____

Please allow 28 days for delivery. Please tick box if you do not wish to receive any additional information   ☐

Prices and availability subject to change without notice.

METHUEN DRAMA
MONOLOGUE & SCENE BOOKS

☐ CONTEMPORARY SCENES FOR ACTORS (MEN)	Earley and Keil	£8.99
☐ CONTEMPORARY SCENES FOR ACTORS (WOMEN)	Earley and Keil	£8.99
☐ THE CLASSICAL MONOLOGUE (MEN)	Earley and Keil	£7.99
☐ THE CLASSICAL MONOLOGUE (WOMEN)	Earley and Keil	£7.99
☐ THE CONTEMPORARY MONOLOGUE (MEN)	Earley and Keil	£7.99
☐ THE CONTEMPORARY MONOLOGUE (WOMEN)	Earley and Keil	£7.99
☐ THE MODERN MONOLOGUE (MEN)	Earley and Keil	£7.99
☐ THE MODERN MONOLOGUE (WOMEN)	Earley and Keil	£7.99
☐ THE METHUEN AUDITION BOOK FOR MEN	Annika Bluhm	£6.99
☐ THE METHUEN AUDITION BOOK FOR WOMEN	Annika Bluhm	£6.99
☐ THE METHUEN AUDITION BOOK FOR YOUNG ACTORS	Anne Harvey	£6.99
☐ THE METHUEN BOOK OF DUOLOGUES FOR YOUNG ACTORS	Anne Harvey	£6.99

● All Methuen Drama books are available through mail order or from your local bookshop.

Please send cheque/eurocheque/postal order (sterling only) Access, Visa, Mastercard, Diners Card, Switch or Amex.

Expiry Date: _____ Signature: _____

Please allow 75 pence per book for post and packing U.K.
Overseas customers please allow £1.00 per copy for post and packing.

ALL ORDERS TO:

Methuen Books, Books by Post, TBS Limited, The Book Service, Colchester Road, Frating Green, Colchester, Essex CO7 7DW.

NAME: _____

ADDRESS: _____

_____

_____

Please allow 28 days for delivery. Please tick box if you do not
wish to receive any additional information ☐

Prices and availability subject to change without notice.

METHUEN STUDENT EDITIONS

☐ SERJEANT MUSGRAVE'S DANCE	John Arden	£6.99
☐ CONFUSIONS	Alan Ayckbourn	£5.99
☐ THE ROVER	Aphra Behn	£5.99
☐ LEAR	Edward Bond	£6.99
☐ THE CAUCASIAN CHALK CIRCLE	Bertolt Brecht	£6.99
☐ MOTHER COURAGE AND HER CHILDREN	Bertolt Brecht	£6.99
☐ THE CHERRY ORCHARD	Anton Chekhov	£5.99
☐ TOP GIRLS	Caryl Churchill	£6.99
☐ A TASTE OF HONEY	Shelagh Delaney	£6.99
☐ STRIFE	John Galsworthy	£5.99
☐ ACROSS OKA	Robert Holman	£5.99
☐ A DOLL'S HOUSE	Henrik Ibsen	£5.99
☐ MY MOTHER SAID I NEVER SHOULD	Charlotte Keatley	£6.99
☐ DREAMS OF ANNE FRANK	Bernard Kops	£5.99
☐ BLOOD WEDDING	Federico Lorca	£5.99
☐ THE MALCONTENT	John Marston	£5.99
☐ BLOOD BROTHERS	Willy Russell	£6.99
☐ DEATH AND THE KING'S HORSEMAN	Wole Soyinka	£6.99
☐ THE PLAYBOY OF THE WESTERN WORLD	J.M. Synge	£5.99
☐ OUR COUNTRY'S GOOD	Timberlake Wertenbaker	£6.99
☐ THE IMPORTANCE OF BEING EARNEST	Oscar Wilde	£5.99
☐ A STREETCAR NAMED DESIRE	Tennessee Williams	£5.99

● All Methuen Drama books are available through mail order or from your local bookshop.

Please send cheque/eurocheque/postal order (sterling only) Access, Visa, Mastercard, Diners Card, Switch or Amex.

☐☐☐☐☐☐☐☐☐☐☐☐☐☐☐☐

Expiry Date:_____ Signature: _____

Please allow 75 pence per book for post and packing U.K.
Overseas customers please allow £1.00 per copy for post and packing.

ALL ORDERS TO:

Methuen Books, Books by Post, TBS Limited, The Book Service, Colchester Road, Frating Green, Colchester, Essex CO7 7DW.

NAME:_____

ADDRESS:_____

_____

Please allow 28 days for delivery. Please tick box if you do not wish to receive any additional information   ☐

Prices and availability subject to change without notice.